SECOND INNINGS

By the Same Author

A CRICKETER'S BOOK

DAYS IN THE SUN

THE SUMMER GAME

CRICKET

GOOD DAYS

AUSTRALIAN SUMMER

ENGLISH CRICKET

TEN COMPOSERS

AUTOBIOGRAPHY

Second Innings

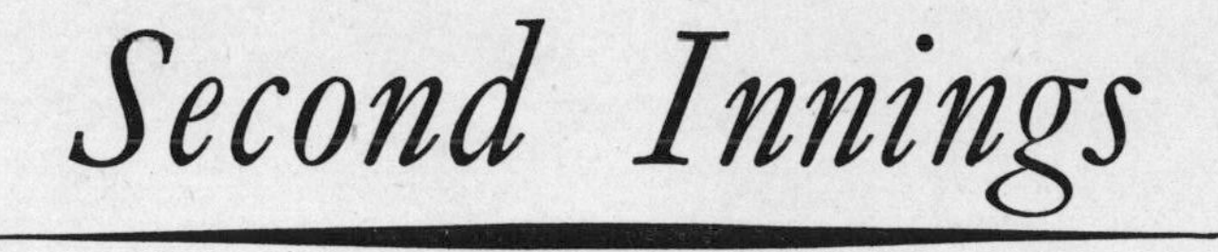

By

NEVILLE CARDUS

COLLINS
ST. JAMES'S PLACE LONDON
1950

PRINTED IN GREAT BRITAIN
COLLINS CLEAR-TYPE PRESS : LONDON AND GLASGOW
1950

To
MY FRIENDS

* I *

THERE was a sequestered purlieu called Victoria Park not more than a half an hour's drive in a carriage from Manchester; the city in those years of the early nineteen-hundreds came to a sudden end on its southern side at the church in Rusholme, near the lane running along the Platt estate, a gracious pleasance with the meadows of Chorlton in the western distance and the village of Fallowfield hidden behind a clump of trees. There were toll-gates at the roads, which gave entrance to Victoria Park; no vehicle not possessed by dwellers within these select groves was admitted free of charge. Pedestrians enjoyed right of way, but, such was the sense of propriety cultivated by the lower orders of the period, none abused the privilege. Victoria Park was the preserve of wealthy German Jews; and the names of most of them were graven on burnished brass at the entrances of counting-houses of Portland Street—Schill Seebohm, Mandelberg, Maurice Spiegelberg, Hertz, Hirschberg. After a Hallé concert conducted by Hans Richter, carriages would make a procession along Oxford Road, every Thursday night, under the damp dripping arch of the railway, up the brow and past All Saints, where a churchyard was denied privacy, though none was perhaps needed now; for time and weather had rendered most of the graves and shattered pillars nameless, without dates or means of identification. Passing slums on the right, and on the left a frontage of shops feebly emulative of Oxford Street in London, including a Frascati's Restaurant, the cavalcade would go its unheeding way until High Street was reached; here was a change of air, a middle-class gentility of stucco, a bridge-passage to the Park itself.

"Carriages at 10" announced the programme of the Hallé Concerts; and they were drawn by good blood-stock, urged on and instructed in the German language. If a "four-wheeler" should be obliged to move in the same direction, plying a habitual and utilitarian trade, the cabby knowing his place would as quickly as possible extricate himself and his hack and get close to the kerb. The ordinary denizen of Manchester, clerk or artisan, or manager of a bank at £500 a year, remembered, if ever he chanced to forget, that this was Hallé Concert night. Not all of the population of this opulent centre of industry and merchandise in the North of England could have told you exactly what went on every week at a Hallé Concert, except that it was "classical" music, mostly German. This was the age in which music was definitely not for the masses; we knew our "Messiah" in Manchester well enough, but the names of Wagner and Tchaikovsky were exclusive and foreign and tentatively pronounced.

Inside Victoria Park, the carriages swung by iron gates and pillars, and curved along drives to massive turreted stone houses, at the base of them broad steps leading up to the portals, flanked by lions *couchant*. There was a brief opening and clapping-to of doors, a clicking of handles, a glimpse into severely upholstered interiors, then the carriage wheels crunched on the gravel again for a while, and soon the thoroughfares of the Park were vacant in the winter blackness ; and none but the policeman witnessed the lights go out after midnight, first in the wide casements looking on the lawns, a little later in the bedrooms above.

I hold a memory of a dining-room in one of these houses, heavy furniture and a *Stambaum* on the wall, a family tree branching like a Banyan, dates and names down the ages from Hanover. On the wall above the sideboard, where a bowl of oranges glowed in the light of wood fire and chandelier, was the portrait of the mother of my host, a gracious old lady, dead long ago in a Germany known for its Gemütlichkeit.

We sat at the polished table and drank a gentle hock. The little professor's wife had retired for the night; there was nobody else in the house except the servants, and they were asleep in their attics. Little Max was the typical German musician of the period, his long hair brushed back over a large brow, tiny lenses in his spectacles, a ragged moustache, a gnome of a man brimming with nature and naïve enthusiasm for his art. He was professor of piano at the college of music in Manchester ; and the principal and presiding genius of the establishment was Dr. Adolf Brodsky, the first to play the Tchaikovsky Violin Concerto. Long years of residence in Manchester lent neither to Max nor to Adolf the accents of our language ; as much German as English was spoken in these homes in Victoria Park, and nearly all the music heard in them was German, though Max favoured Grieg, whom he knew and tried to resemble in appearance.

Outside I heard the wind in the trees. I remembered that when a boy I had got up early on autumn mornings after a gale in the night to go out before nine o'clock school to look with other boys for fuel for November the Fifth. It was in Victoria Park we would search for our most substantial hauls, great snapped-off branches; and we would drag them through the streets and store them for the bonfire night. As silence fell on our conversation in Max's dining-room, I heard the creaking of branches outside. A log in the fire collapsed and the flames and sparks renewed heat and glow, and they were reflected in another portrait, this one over the fireplace—Max's father, and Max was so much like him now that it might easily have been himself. Dead, too, like his mother. And Max had no children.

He spoke of his art as it is seldom spoken of nowadays. Performance was then a means to an end, the making of music. It was a natural part of intercourse between friends, not a public and abnormal achievement. "Last night Brodsky vos here," said Max; "and we play the G major Brahms Sonate; we bofe play it vonce before Brahms himself. And when we haf played, Brodsky he sits down, choost a little 'ot and short of breath; then he stand up immediate, and he says, 'Noch einmal, Max;' again we play it, *now*, it is so lofely!" He laughed until tears compelled him to take off his spectacles and wipe them. "More wine?" he said.

Suddenly I felt the pathos of the scene and the hour. The warm hearth, the portraits on the wall and the sleepers upstairs, the delicate stems of the wine-glasses, the gleam of the oranges on the sideboard; all so tangible and corporeal at this moment of enjoyment. But it was passing; I could hear and feel it vanishing, vanishing now, for all my absorption in the physical as well as the æsthetic reality.

At last I have to go. Max is obviously getting tired. He helps me into my overcoat in the hall, and talks of a cab, but I prefer to walk. He shakes my hand with both of his. As I walk down the drive, I hear him chaining and locking the door. Through the rhododendrons I can see a solitary statue dim but gleaming in the night. . . . For all the years afterwards my supper with Max, at the end of a Hallé Concert, has crystallised for me a set of emotions and sensibilities from which to find an attitude to life, with the mind clarifying opacities of far-off experiences felt and seen. As I look back on this evening a whole world of removed beauty is recalled just for a moment of time.

The houses in Victoria Park are to-day mostly nursing-homes. A tramway clangs through the main thoroughfare; the toll-gates have long since been democratically abolished. No small boys go there early on autumn mornings, looking for wood for the burning of Guy Fawkes, broken branches after the gale in the night.

I remember a little round glass globe with a castle

inside and a fir-tree; when it was shaken white snow filled all the world; nothing was to be seen but whirling snow, then it would slowly settle down at the bottom of the globe and the castle and the fir-tree came into sight again, standing there alone and quiet. It was one of my first pleasures in life to sit shaking my magic globe, but often I would hold it in my hands very still so that I could look into it and see no sign of life; it was as another element, a realm of silence and enchantment. I would think myself, will myself, inside the globe, not my body—which would have intruded—but my dreams, my imagination.

Snow glistens in all the memory's of one's boyhood. Outside the window it falls and we try to single out one flake and follow it down to the ground. We press our noses flat to the window-pane, and our breath hides the view for a while. There was a song we would chant on these days of stealthily falling snow, snow thickening minute by minute.

Snow snow faster
Ala-alabaster.

Or we would say it was Mother Goose plucking feathers. The snow widened the city's streets; they became spacious, with no confining edges. But for a long time the snow would not "stick" on the pavements; I would sit at the window waiting for it to stay on the ground and not melt. I would go to the door and hold out my hand to assure myself that the snow had not ceased falling; and in my open palm a flake fell like something alive which tickled me. It was a game to catch and hold just one of the millions of whirling and fluttering little visitants from the heavens, to catch and hold it for a second of time; for swiftly it was changed to a spot of moisture and I would sip it into my mouth and pretend that it was a magic potion, and half expect something wonderful to happen to me. With countless other boys since the world began I looked up to the sky and thought of all the loads of snow up there being emptied out of the clouds.

A scene returns to me now, as I write. I knelt on a chair to enable me to peep through the lace curtains of the window: a long vista of steadily descending flakes, and across the way was a solitary figure playing a trumpet, a street musician. The hollow notes and the falling snow filled me with a melancholy beyond a boy's understanding, even a grown man's. To see snow beginning to fall, to see almost the first flake through the window on a December afternoon, this was a strange and secret delight. The next best wonder was to wake in the morning, an hour before breakfast and school, and listen for the familiar sounds outside, footsteps and the wheels of milk-carts and the clop of a horse's hoofs, and to hear nothing. The bedroom would be full of white light. Then as we looked through the window we saw snow, thick and smooth everywhere, only the chimney stacks as real as usual; or perhaps in the backyard the handle of a shovel reared starkly upward, leaning against the wall, the rest of the implement buried.

The dog would dash out of the house impetuous as

usual at the opening of the front door. For a fraction of a second you could sense his astonishment at what he saw and experienced, an endless habitation of strange whiteness. He would put his nose into the snow and snuffle. The cat, on the contrary, would inspect the phenomena from the doorstep, one paw gingerly uplifted. In the swift passing of time between leaving home for school and getting there, what a hurried pulsation of experience !—the first thrust of the hands into the cold powder to make a snowball, and the massaging of it into some hardness, to lend solidity and "carrying power." I lived in mortal fear of receiving a snowball flat in the face; and the suspense of turning a street corner was only slightly lessened if I made a long detour, cutting off sharp angles of walls. I am certain that no snow falls nowadays as it did then; and even if it does we are no longer young enough to enjoy it. We have grown old as soon as we think of the thaw after snow-fall. Old age, in fact, sets in as soon as we take note of changes in the wind and think of wet feet. It was my delight to walk in puddles. I would seek out the deepest. The great thing was to get the water over the boots, to lose sight of the boots altogether. Also there was the joy of bending the boot to make squelching noises.

But no boy ever liked to know that a thaw was at hand. With the minimum amount of snow we tried to make a snowball, rolling and rolling a tiny handful along the earth, persistently, patiently, until the blood was in our heads. Given a huge fall of snow, there was a snowman to build, almost a monument, pieces of coal for the eyes and mouth, an upturned bucket for the hat, and a twig off a tree for his pipe.

As the afternoon passed to twilight, the glow of firesides deepened to a warmer security because of the hardening snow outside, as the frost bound the city into steel. Not for years did I know of the countryside under snow; I lived in Manchester through all my boyhood. But I do not believe that there is as much pleasure for a boy in snowfalls in the countryside as in the city, where lighted thoroughfares and shops make a romantic contrast to the invasion from the winter sky; the muffling of traffic, the hurrying people all growing whiter on their hats and shoulders and their shirt fronts; a transformation scene, a change from dull and grimy reality into a fairyland. I once saw a lamplighter in the snow, moving silently along the pavement, putting up his long pole, and he revealed the dancing flakes above, circling and hovering in the illumination.

Did it always snow at Christmas when we were young? I cannot—or at least I will not—remember a "green" Christmas, a Christmas of rain and fog. The covers of the illustrated papers and "double numbers" turned the nurseries into a glory of holly and robin redbreast and stage-coaches and rosy inns and coachmen with pleated capes. Snow at Christmas makes the clock go back; it touches everything with a medieval spirit, mingling jollity and the grotesque; "God Rest Ye Merry, Gentlemen," and "The Mistletoe Bough"; brandy flames round the pudding and ghost stories. If Christmas Eve should be white and moonlit, the star of mysticism may be seen to shine over even an English

Christmas; for the English Christmas is one less of poetry than of hospitable prose.

When the meadows froze, people would hunt out skates, wooden and steel. The rivers and ponds were a mass of moving figures. At any moment the weight of them threatened a crash and splintering of ice. Elderly men with mufflers over their shoulders puffing out their breath on the cold air. Boys and girls, young men escorting young ladies, their skates rhythmically keeping time. Then there were "slides," on which a perpetual queue proceeded in various attitudes of arrested animation; some dashing along legs wide asunder, others as though human volition were gone—once landed on a slide there was little freedom of the will and much stiffness at the knee-joints; and as you glided forward, or rather were subtly propelled, there was always the feeling that the person behind you was inimical, at least not friendly.

The sky lowered and the sun became a smoky red globe. The weather-wise would glance upward and say "Plenty more to come." At home, after the icicles of the east wind as the twilight fell, there was the fire-side waiting, the kettle singing on the hob, and the smell of slightly burnt toast.

Then the Christmas pantomime. I once stole out of my home and without a word to anybody went to an afternoon performance of *Aladdin*. I climbed to the high gallery of the Prince's Theatre in Manchester, admission sixpence. While I sat aloft, and looked down on all the kingdoms of the world, time came to a stand-still, and outside the afternoon turned to night. When the spell was broken I found myself in the Oxford Road; snow was falling. There had been no warning of it when I had entered the theatre. I had sat in the gallery trembling with excitement as one scene was conjured from another. All the time, behind my back, the snow had come to a great city on the eve of Christmas.

Under a clear moon and a sky pulsing with stars as though frosted, I was once allowed to go out with the Christmas "Waits" singing carols. I carried a lantern which was like a little castle; through a skin of parchment it was possible to see the wick inside burning steadily. The glow thrown upward by the lamps set into relief the faces of the singers; and I remember an old man with a beard like Christ; the shadows on his cheeks and under his eyes made me think of a picture I loved—Holman Hunt's "The Light of the World." The snow was hard under our feet. When we walked up the drives of houses in Victoria Park we made crunching noises, and we spoke in whispers as we prepared to sing outside the wide porches. There was a desire amongst us that the carols should be heard inside the houses without warning: it was a seasonal ritual and greeting.

Christians awake!
Salute the happy morn!

After a while, long enough to suggest that our music had been listened to for its own sake, the door would open and we would be asked to come inside. It was this way, I think, that I first saw a large gleaming dining-room and old furniture, a chandelier, a crackling log-fire, a sideboard with decanters and glasses and fruit and silver-rimmed biscuit boxes. Our host might easily have been little Max himself, not old yet, with many Christmases still before him.

I was not allowed to stay out all through the night and go with the " Waits " from house to house until Christmas morning dawned; but in my little bedroom at home I would wake very early and grope for my stocking and try to guess without lighting a candle what was it in. And I would hear, from the distance, now near on the wind and now far, the cheerful greeting:

Hail smiling morn,
That tips the hills with gold!

Snow on the roofs, in the streets and in the fields beyond, a mantle of peacefulness. Snow falling and snow dissolving, as imperceptibly as all these happy hours were vanishing and passing on their way. At no point could we detect a transition, increase or decrease; nobody ever saw the first or the last flake of a snowstorm. So, like to the falling snow, in which no flake is different from another, or more laden with fate or change—so with our myriad lives and the whole of our world of those days. Peace on earth, goodwill towards all men. Where was the mortal heart that didn't believe it? No man envies another and would take his place; yet the years blow us here and there, and we are sent drifting on winds as wayward as those that swing the weather-vane on the snowy roof.

It was in snow and at Christmas that I once travelled through the Tyrol from Innsbruck to Vienna. All that happened on what was a normal and uneventful journey was subsequently enclosed in the magic-glass globe of memory. At the dawn of Christmas I peeped through the curtains of my sleeping car and saw a village, at the foot of a great mountain; it was awakening in a gentle twinkle of lights. I saw a dog pulling a sleigh. I caught a glimpse through a window just unshuttered of an old peasant woman looking out at the passing train, over the snow. Another morning on the endless drift of the years while the stars waned, a brief glimpse into lives that would never touch mine. Everywhere the unsmutched snow and a sense of the mystical presence of manger and oxen, while the light of day glimmered. Soon the train was out of sight of the village, and there was nothing but snow far and wide, snow falling without haste, obliterating in a moment the marks of a sparrow's feet on a branch of a tree.

All day long the snow seemed to bless the country through which we journeyed; there was no malice in its soft whiteness. Out of drift the fir-trees emerged, and they looked like cones with ice-cream generously dropping over.

In Vienna the snow was piled in high walls along the edges of the pathways in the Ringstrasse and the Schottenring. At night the two spires of the Votifkirche were as though made of powdered glass or stardust; a single puff of breath would blow them away. The air was keen as a knife; in my heated bedroom in the Regina Hotel I tried to open the double-window, in the name of ventilation. I shut it swift as a guillotine as soon as I felt the first inrush of fangs and spears of cold. Old women, their bare feet wrapped round with straw, swept the pavements in vain. The entire city was as though under a veil; its motion and scarcely visible life were the spots of the veil; there was more white and black, a swirling veil over all and everything. In the restaurant of the hotel were warmth and wine; the time of day was lunch, and through the swing-door, heavily curtained against draughts, a tall man walked from the street, fur on his coat-collar. He removed a black wide-brimmed hat and also he took off his horn-rimmed spectacles for a moment because the sudden change of temperature had covered them with moisture. Then he put them on, looked around and strode to a table where, amongst others, sat a beautiful girl. He took her hand, kissed it, and sang the first phrase of Brahms's "Wie bist du meine Königin." Old Kremslehner, the proprietor of the hotel, came to my table, looking very like Anton Bruckner. With a low bow he said to me in English, "Good morning, how you are?" Every time I lunched and dined in the restaurant he repeated the gesture and the phrase. At the reception office there was Fritz, pasty-faced, with a little blonde moustache and mild eyes, and green apron, always doing six things at once, answering a telephone, handing out bedroom keys, or looking for letters through piles of them; always there from morning till night. One day he did not appear behind his counter until towards noon. He had been taken ill while shaving, not seriously, he told me—he would never allow me to speak with him except in English. "I was suddenly—suddenly . . ." He groped for the word. "What is it?—ach, it is annoying; I know it so well—schwindelig—no, plis, don't tell me; I shall remember it later and tell you." I did not come back to the hotel until after midnight; I heard "Die Frau ohne Schatten" of Strauss at the opera, Strauss conducting, quietly, efficiently, his great forehead bent over the score; but on the stage there was such a stain of colour in Barak the dyer's house that I forgot the snow, and in the *entr'acte* Buxbaum played his 'cello with tearful romance; and the taxi-driver who brought me through the blizzard—for no longer was it merely a snowstorm—found time to ask how the Lehmann had sung, and he beamed when I said "Schön—herrlich!" As soon as I entered the hotel vestibule, Fritz shouted at me in uncontrollable excitement and triumph, "Deezy—that was the word, Herr Cardus—dee-zy." I have seldom seen a man so happy.

On the night of Christmas, Schalk conducted *Die Meistersinger*, and the opera house was as animated off the stage as during the apprentice scenes on it; for there were children everywhere, and they not only revelled in David and the belabouring of Beckmesser; they were quiet as mice when Sachs pored over his great tome and sighed out his "Wahn, wahn, überall wahn!" Most of them had been only babies when the war of 1918 began; they were now about to come under the shadow of another war. "Gott weiss wie das geschah!" sang Friedrich Schorr on this evening of Christmas in 1924, while the snow covered the city and the countryside, blanketed the Prater, and eddied about the weathercocks in Grinzing, and dropped from the signposts as in the "Winterreise" of Schubert long ago.

It all happened in a time so distant and irreclaimable that I can scarcely believe I did not see it all taking place in the glass globe which I would look into and shake when I was a boy.

* II *

I WAS not more than twelve years old when I first entered a theatre. It was one of Robert Courtneidge's Christmas pantomimes in Manchester, *Robinson Crusoe*, I think, with Vesta Tilley as the principal boy. I was not "taken" to this pantomime; I went by myself and watched from the highest gallery in the world, after long waiting in a queue until you would hear the lifting of a bar at the door. You placed your sixpence under a wire-netting, from behind which the girl or woman in charge pressed a lever, and a heavy square deposit of lead came out of a slot. That was your ticket.

The climb to the gallery was arduous, even to an eager boy. Round and round, with acute angles all the way; at every step upwards one's body became more bent to the purpose, the knee action more deliberate, the breath more sternly drawn. Then, at the top of the steps was a dark refreshment bar (not yet opened) to pass through, and now at last the theatre itself was attained. At great distance below was the stage, the curtain alluringly down. To find a front place in the gallery involved some agility and nerve; there were no seats, only long rows of wooden ledges, and to save time and to get there first we did not walk gingerly down a central staircase but leaped from cliff to cliff. We would lean over the rail of the gallery and watch the stalls and pit assembling. Sometimes a programme fluttered down, like a visitant from another hemisphere.

When I write that "we" would lean over the gallery rail, I am using the "we" metaphorically; for I went alone to the theatre in my boyhood, as indeed I went alone everywhere, walking through the city streets reading a boy's paper and by some instinct always coming out of my enchantment just in time not to bump against a lamp-post. I do not know how I contrived to get money for admission to the theatre gallery week by week; on one occasion at least I committed petty theft. I stole a volume out of the limited and discursive family library, which comprised *East Lynne*, the Bible, somebody's Dream Book, and one other novel, this by Marion Crawford. The volume I stole was a collection of poems by Coleridge, and I am at a loss to this day to understand how it came to find a place in the household. I took it to a second-hand bookseller's in Oxford Street owned by a man of immeasurable age, who made me think of the Old Testament. His clothes were shiny and he smelt; his name was Coleman; and in his front window, amongst a ruin of ancient literature, was a phrenologist's bust, the head marked into squares like the counties on a map. The interior of the shop was gloomy; piles of books, and the odour of damp and slow decay. There was another Coleman, reputed to be a son, with skin of vellum and eyes tightly stuck together by what my fearful imagination visualised as blindness.

Coleman senior looked at the Coleridge, rumbled in his stomach, and offered me a shilling. I took it and fled straight up the brow of Oxford Street, under the railway arch, past the corner shop with birds in cages around the door and gold-fish in globes in the window. It was Saturday afternoon; there was a pantomime matinée. It may have been the sale of Coleridge that enabled me to see Ada Reeve as Aladdin, G. P. Huntley as Widow Twankey, and Horace Mills as Abanazar. I did not go to the pantomime in the innocence of most boys of ten or eleven years old. In those days boys and girls were not encouraged to enter a theatre at all in a provincial English city; the pantomimes of the period were severely sophisticated in their outlook both towards the particular theme of *Cinderella* or *The Forty Thieves* and towards life in general. Maggie Duggan and George Robey occasioned much concern in the councils of the Manchester Watch Committee, protectors of public morals. There was also a suspicion in many families that theatres were peculiarly combustible and likely to catch fire; in brief, for a boy to set foot in a theatre alone was thought a certain means sooner or later either of going to the devil or of being burnt alive. The danger to my morals seldom occurred to me, but frequently I felt a vague apprehensiveness when I stood looking down over the gallery rail on the delights below, forbidden delights, delights deceitfully enjoyed; for I always lied whenever I was asked where I had been when I got home again. Electricity was more or less a new and experimental department of science forty years ago; and Robert Courtneidge invariably brought the first part of his pantomime to an end by a long "transformation" scene, in which furnaces of magnificences were unfolded as one flimsy gauze curtain after another ascended on high, beginning with the narrowest strip of the stage on which the Fairy Queen stood, in company with the principal boy; and she would wave her wand saying:

And now Aladdin take me by the hand
And I will show you all the joys of Fairyland.

Opalescent deeps of the sea; caves of turquoise and rubies; apocalyptic sunrises and radiance of every boy's dream of the Arabian Nights, all accumulating in a lavish expense of electricity. It was with an amount of relief that one witnessed at the apotheosis a temporary lowering of the fireproof curtain.

As I say, I did not attend my pantomimes in the innocence of childhood; the fairy-tale basis of a pantomime had for me but a secondary interest. I marked the distinction between Robinson Crusoe and the principal boy who happened to be playing the part; I knew that Abanazar was Horace Mills, and once when I saw Horace Mills walking in a Manchester Street looking exactly like any man of business wearing gloves and a bowler hat, I followed secretly behind him and laughed to myself at his every movement, though he did nothing that was the slightest bit funny off the stage. Ada Reeve was Aladdin one year; I remember that when she couldn't remember the word "Abracadabra," and she realised she was locked in the cave more or less for ever, she immediately consoled herself and the rest of us by singing "Good-bye, Dolly Gray," the popular song of the Boer War. But the point is that she didn't sing the chorus but spoke it, in a husky dramatic monotone. This was revolutionary; this was new method. The cognoscenti in the dress circle, I was informed years afterwards, were taken aback, and they shook their heads until by force of art Ada Reeve conquered a lifetime's principles. Round about this time of my life I saw Ada Reeve in *Floradora* the very week after the last performance of the pantomime; and pantomime ran from Christmas to Easter; and now she was a fashionable society darling, in a big brimmed hat, and she sang a song called "Tact" in front of a row of long-trousered top-hatted young men with silver-mounted walking sticks. One week Aladdin's cave and the splendour of the Orient, but in a few evenings it had all gone. Now, living and moving and having being on the same boards, walking in the same places where Widow Twankey and Abanazar had shaken the theatre into reckless and eternal laughter, were elegance and romance in a setting of tea-planters or what not; palm trees and deodar, and the melodies of Leslie Stuart. The palimpsest of the stage! I didn't know of such a word but I remember a sudden feeling of sadness coming to my eyes when, once at a pantomime somebody sang "Is your Mammy always with you?" and as I looked at the singer's movements in the round circles of limelight that followed her, throwing two dancing shadows, the thought came to my mind that some day somebody else would perhaps be dancing on the same spot, and all would have become different; all would then be new and this would be forgotten long ago.

The old pantomimes observed a strict set of unities; the identity and comparative importance of the author of the "book"—as it was called—was recognised. The "book" was composed mainly in rhymed couplets, more or less heroic, uttered by the Demon (or Storm) King:

Ride on thou proud and saucy ship
But soon I'll have this Crusoe in my grip.

These lines were invariably pronounced at the beginning of Act 1 in Davy Jones's Locker, which was a drop-scene calling for merely what Mrs. Gamp would have called a "parapidge" of stage. The Demon King was a baritone, and the chances might be that we had last heard him on the pier in August at Southend singing the "Bedouin Love Song" with the pierrots. Now in a more dramatic environment under the sea and in the dark he probably struck a deeper and more ambitious vocal note; "Rage thou angry storm" from Balfe was not beyond the dream of possibility.

An inviolate decree held that in the programmes of classical pantomime the *dramatis personæ* and the cast should be denoted and set forth in a running parenthesis of wit, such as:

Mrs. Sinbad (*who has sin-badder days*) . . . *George Robey.*

From the murky element of the Storm King we would

be changed in the twinkling of an eye to Pekin (maybe); or if the pantomime were of the Occident the scene would be the village green outside the "Bull and Bush." It was in Scene 2 that the pantomime really began and the stalls filled up. The Storm King didn't appear again for hours, or the Fairy Queen. I often wondered what they were doing all the time. In Scene 2 the important personages of the pantomime made their appearance in order of renown. The Baron (or the Emperor) was allowed to hold the centre of the stage for a few minutes; perhaps he was even given a song, but nobody listened to him; he was merely a part of the connived plot of suspense. First came the principal girl—Amy Augarde or even Gertie Millar; then the more substantial principal boy (the best of all was Ada Blanche); and the principal boy would dash down the footlights and embrace the principal girl, kicking his left leg backwards as he did so.

At last, when the "House Full" boards were put up in the theatre's main entrances—terrible to see if you were outside in the fog trying to catch a glimpse of something behind the brilliant lights of the *foyer*—now was the moment: the stage was left significantly vacant for a brief pause. From the wings came sounds of brawl and derision and racket. And the Dame would arrive in some state of dishevelment, out of breath, having, for some reason never explained, been chased. Dan Leno or Robey or Harry Randall or Wilkie Bard—it might be any of them!—in elastic-sided boots, hair parted straight down the middle and tied in a bun, towards which the right hand would absent-mindedly stray when she came down the stage and spoke to us intimately about " Her First " and of the viccisitudes of matrimony. An incomparable school of great English comic-actors created a Dickensian gallery of Dames. The greatest of them was Robey's " Mother Goose," who swerved from the unities of pantomime in her entrance to that most matchless of all pantomimes at the Manchester Theatre Royal, Christmas, 1904; and I saw it many times before it vanished into air the following March.

The scene was Mother Goose's cottage, and the Landlord had called for the rent. George Bastow was Mother Goose's son, and he endeavoured to keep the enemy at bay. (All landlords in our pantomimes and melodramas were enemies, as a matter of democratic course.) " The rent was not paid last week, or the week before, or the week before," raged the tyrant; " this is the last straw and final notice. Into the streets you all go!" At this moment George Robey appeared, bland, with kindly recognition, wiping imaginary soap-suds from the hands on an apron. " Ah, *there* you are, landlord!" said Mother Goose in Robey's fruitiest voice; " *there* you are—such a lot wants doing to the house!"

It was in this same pantomime that George Robey held the stage for half an hour (while the scene-shifters were noisy and active behind a drop-scene, often causing it to bulge from contact with some royal dome or pinnacle) and created the immortal Mrs. Moggeridge, a next-door neighbour, who, because never seen, has lived for ever. Robey came on from the side of the stage in a condition of agitation, fingers twitching, nose sniffing. He cast glances to the direction whence he had entered; they were glances poignant with contumely and injured pride. Simmering a little, but still on the boil, he folded arms, gave another toss of his head sideways and said, simply but obliquely, "Mrs. Moggeridge!" Nothing more than her name to begin with, but the intonation, with a descent of pitch at "ridge," was contemptuous. Then he bent to us over the footlights, and in a sudden hysteria of ridicule, stated (or rather he conveyed) this information: "Fairy Queen in a Christmas pantomime!" After another snort and a pause he added, in a voice pitched to a deeper note of irony, "Her!"

Satisfaction and triumph here became evident in Robey's eyes and gestures; but suddenly he stiffened, and the neck was thrust again towards Mrs. Moggeridge's garden wall, whence obviously some Parthian thrust had been aimed. "And what of it?" asked Robey, the voice rising in mingled menace, disdain and clear conscience. "What of it?" (pronounced "What arv ert").

Speculation sought in vain to deduce the nature of Mrs. Moggeridge's innuendo that it should have compelled this final bridling and this unanswerable fiat. Enough to say that after the pronouncement of it Mrs. Moggeridge was heard no more. It is hard to believe we did not actually hear her or see her; there wasn't never indeed "no sich a person"; it was a conjuration of comic art.

Robey was a master of tantrums, or in other circumstances, of spasms. In *Jack and the Beanstalk*, when

Jack returned home with beans for the sale of the cow, Robey as the Dame achieved an awe-inspiring expression of twitching incredulity, woe and mortification, all evenly blended. He (or she) hurled the beans through the window, and at once the stalk began to grow upward. Robey caught sight of it out of the corner of his eyes as he was suffering another wave of distress. And he began to giggle, to experience hysteria . . . but no words can describe this masterpiece of comic acting. It was done by imaginative absorption into a character and a scene; and here is the difference between the old great pantomime comedians of my youth and the comedians of to-day, who get their laughs by the things they say and are not funny in themselves, and are certainly not actors. Robey and Leno and Wilkie Bard and Little Tich and Harry Weldon were most nights in the year performers in the music-hall, red-nosed and holding an audience for three-quarters of an hour, holding the theatre single-handed, with song and patter; and from time to time they would leave the stage to return as a new character—Robey's Lord Mayor of Muckemdyke, Leno's pathetic little Cockney just married, the victim of a building society; he had bought a house, and he leant over the footlights to tell us in husky confidence of his pride of possession. It was a nice house, with the river at the bottom of the garden; that is, when the garden wasn't at the bottom of the river. But I must use a platitude now; it was not what these old drolls said, it was the way they said it. Little Tich, breathing on his tall hat before giving it a rub round with his elbow, made a noise that emptied his lungs, fraught with bronchitis. Gusto and faith in a complete surrender to extravagance; no smart-cracks but natural nonsense —as when the Ugly Sisters in *Cinderella*, having been refused admission at the ball, Tom Foy said to Malcolm Scott, "Let's walk in backwards and they'll think we're coming out." It was these comedians of the music-hall who peopled our memories of pantomime with a gallery of Dames, each as rich in identity as Betsy Prig and Mrs. Gamp and the nurse in *Romeo and Juliet*.

The convention of pantomime persisted that the Dame and her son should begin poor and end wealthy. All the good characters, in fact, shared ample fortune as a reward of virtue; and during the last scene they came before us most opulently garbed—Robey's magnificence was like a fantastic dream or apotheosis of a riotously lunatic Schiarapelli. The lesser male luminaries of the show, Idle Jack or Tinbad the Tailor, would wear terrific check suits with huge buttons of gold, and their choice in walking sticks was *rococo*. Nobody was harshly treated in this last of all the pantomime's consummations of glory and electricity; even the Demon King received a burst of applause when he appeared, apparently a reformed character, in morning-coat and grey topper. And the children crowed their delight as the Cat came on for his share of the general recognition and acclamation, wearing a fur coat most likely.

Then the final chorus and the last ruthless descent of the curtain. Nothing left but the return to the world, to find oneself again in the streets outside, where life had been going on just the same on a winter day; it was dark now, with the gas-lamps burning, and when we had entered in realms of gold it had been afternoon and broad daylight.

In the street at the back of the Manchester Theatre Royal was a long narrow door through which the scenery was carried to the stage. At night I would go there, when nobody was looking, and peep through the slit and try to catch the glimpse of the magic interior. I would hear the pantomime in the distance, the laughter and the striking up of the band; and I knew exactly what was happening at this moment—Daisy Jerome was coming on to the stage as a Dutch girl in sabots and stamping them with stiff ankles and singing something about diamonds in Amsterdam, Amsterdam, Amsterdam. I knew the pantomime word and music perfect, with all the patter and action, so that on any afternoon or evening wherever I happened to be—probably walking the Manchester streets—I could follow any performance and live in it by proxy, so to say. As I mumbled to myself and imitated Robey's eyebrows and bulging cheeks, I was probably regarded by passers-by as an idiot boy.

Joy beyond the dream of avarice came to me when I obtained a job selling chocolates in the Comedy Theatre, where Eugene Stratton was Pete the page-boy in *Cinderella*. Every afternoon at two o'clock, every evening at seven, for three months—and I could see it all for nothing, in fact was actually paid a few shillings weekly. I would ply my trade until the curtain rose, then stand at the side of the pit, my tray still strapped over my shoulders, and as time went on I acquired a professional casualness, even to the point of leaving the auditorium during certain of the less momentous scenes, and going into the bar to count my proceeds and replenish stock in time for the interval. I would contemplate the audience, the majority of them new to the show, with the tolerance of the " deadhead " towards the *dilettante* ; if the principal boy happened to be below her best form I could put a proper value on loose uninstructed applause.

I was actually spoken to once by Eugene Stratton, who came through a door covered with green baize into the front of the theatre after a matinée. He wore a tweed overcoat and a soft hat and he called me " Sonny." He was a little man with a careworn but kindly face, and he had about him a strange odour of limelight and Havana cigar. It was in this pantomime that Stratton presented his " scena " of the negro horse thief, " I may be crazy, but I love you." " So won't you come right here and say good-bye, bekase I may not see you any more." He stood with his slouch hat hanging down from his right hand, looking at the bedroom window of the shack where his lady-love dwelt ; he lifted himself slightly on tip-toe to get his high notes.

When at last the pantomime came to an end winter was changing to spring. On the Monday following the last performance on a Saturday night, I was a wandering spirit. The theatre was closed, and I walked about the streets, melancholy in the twilight. The cloud-capped towers and the gorgeous palaces, the great globe itself, had dissolved. The principal girl, whose portrait on a post-card I had carried in my pocket since Christmas, until the edges frayed, was far away in London, rehearsing for a George Edwardes' musical comedy. Stratton was top of the bill at the Hippodrome in Newcastle. The Fairy Queen had returned to her home in Balham, where her invalid mother lived. On the front page of *The Era* was a brief statement to the effect that the Demon King was " resting " in Acacia Road or Maida Vale.

Pain which I could not define came into my heart and stomach when I wondered where at this very minute all the scattered glories might chance to be. The dispersion of forces brought together, God knows how, for a moment !—no, I was not sophisticated enough to understand this ironic flavour in my boyish sense of loss, as the old pantomimes dispersed, or whenever school broke up and the playing-fields stood empty in the evening's afterglow and I thought of all I had known there only a day or two since, and everybody somewhere in a void to-night.

So with the high galleries of the theatres from which I looked down and experienced hours of happiness which, while they were passing, cheated us into believing they were far beyond the touch of time. Absorbed in pleasure, the romance and tinsel of the stage entering the mind and blood like a medieval chemist's magic distillation. Applause that came from rapture and love—for we loved those that played for us week by week. And at the last night we sang from gallery and pit and circle and stalls " Shall Auld Acquaintance be Forgot ; " and Mother Goose and the Demon King and her son Jack and the Principal Boy and the Baron and the Fairy Queen held crossed hands and jerked them to the tune's rhythm, before the last inexorably obliterating curtain.

After one such farewell I went the next evening into a Manchester park, and sat on a bench and tried to read a book. My imagination winged the entire face of England looking and listening. Then the bell tolled, announcing the time for the closing of the gates, and the pathways became misty and vacant and I heard the park-keeper's cry " All out, all out ! " From another direction came echoes : " All out, all out ! " In the smouldering Manchester sunset I tried to see the symbol of London and all its lights ; Shaftesbury Avenue and Leicester Square—and Drury Lane itself, where the Christmas pantomime was even yet, in late March, running twice daily, though the boards were up announcing the " Last Weeks," and the confectioners' shop windows were already full of Easter eggs.

* III *

WHEN I was a boy I read nothing except school and adventure stories, in publications from the House of Harmsworth,—Alfred Harmsworth, later Lord Northcliffe, who realised shrewdly and quickly that a lower-class youth was rising from a poor respectability, rather above devouring the out-and-out penny dreadful of the period, yet a youth that would not go as far as a ready acceptance of the *Boy's Own Paper*, which was obviously for the sons of gentlemen. Harmsworth, in *The Boy's Friend*, appealed to the products of the council or " board schools " ; this paper gave us school stories in which the atmosphere of Talbot Baines Reed was rendered accommodatingly urban and not too esoteric for readers whose social ambitions concentrated on escape from the artisan to the clerkly stratum.

I was not allowed, even in my semi-literate home, to read about Deadwood Dick in a frankly lurid paper called *Pluck*, also a Harmsworth publication, for his net was generously flung ; my first sense of mortal sin came to me when one night I stole to bed with a candle in my pocket and *Pluck*, and in a dim light encouraged at the age of thirteen a galloping myopia. I would read with my held breath, the bedclothes drawn over me like a curtain, almost as though to conceal from the eye of God Himself what I was doing. One night my grandmother came suddenly into the room and I pushed the " dreadful " under my pillow, picked up a school textbook and said I was preparing a lesson. As far as I can remember, this was the first deception I ever practised unrepentantly. But *The Boy's Friend* was not included on the family index of pernicious and demoralising literature, probably because it contained school stories by an author named Henry St. John, and also because it was edited by one named Hamilton Edwardes, a drawing of whom appeared at the top of a column called " From My Den." This drawing depicted a man definitely aristocratic of mien, in a well-stocked library. In the school stories of Henry St. John the masters were presented as the sworn enemies of the boys, which was a refreshing change from and truer to life than " Eric, or Little by Little," by Dean Farrar, a gilt-bound volume used as a school prize, in which the boys were friendly with the masters to the point of taking tea with them on Sunday afternoons and discussing their futures, here and in the world to come. I objected to all improving stories on principle. I would not read Jules Verne because I felt that behind the show of exciting escapades in balloons and submarines twenty thousand leagues under the sea some sort of scientific instruction was going on. I fought shy of Henty too ; I suspected him of geography. Hamilton Edwardes each week addressed his " dear readers," man to man, and from time to time he would take us into a sort of professional confidence and tell us he had recently been kept up all night perusing the MS. of a new school story by Henry St. John—a "ripping" one, far more engrossing than any even this author had ever before written; and the first instalment would appear in a few weeks, so please order from your newsagent a copy of *The Boy's Friend* to be delivered to your home every Wednesday morning without fail.

Henry St. John's boys were dressed in Eton collars and jackets, but we could easily recognise them as of our own breed and speech; they used onomatopœia, such as "Hellup! Ouch! Phew! Snakes!" The French master was invariably called Froggie; and he wore a cape and a tall hat that narrowed towards the top. The extent of his French ranged from "Nom de pipe!" to "Ma foi!" Sometimes he came under the suspicion of being a spy; apparently the time devoted to Learning in Henry St. John's public schools was scanty and fortuitous.

Harmsworth's principal authors of adventure serials were Maxwell Scott, who invented Nelson Lee the detective; and Sydney Drew, "creator," as Hamilton Edwardes called him, of Ferrers Lord the millionaire who built a submarine that could also fly and became master of the air and the sea, and of course disclosed his formula to the British Government in a moment of severe international crisis. In the walks of fiction explored by *The Boy's Friend* no allusion was ever made to women or to any females of any age whatsoever, young or old, except maybe to the matron in the tuck-shop at Repminster School. If any boy of Henry St. John's fancy referred merely to his sister, he was promptly called "spooney" by his companions. In the more mature universes of Maxwell Scott's and Sydney Drew's imagination, the men were dedicated wholly and austerely to celibacy; their various activities seemed to give them no time for anything else. Even at the end of a serial, when Ferrers Lord or Nelson Lee had come triumphantly to fame and full accomplishment of the task they had put their hand to, when villainy had been vanquished, they did not marry and live happily ever afterwards. The author reserved to himself the right to use them again in any sequel demanded by Hamilton Edwardes at any future time, according to taste, circulation and public demand.

The Boy's Friend was printed on green paper and the pages were large and there were apparently an abundance of them when each Wednesday morning I would surrender myself to its allurements. Seldom in after life have I known literature to cast so potent a spell as this. At the end of a "thrilling" instalment, I would be brought up with a shock by the words "To be continued next week"; and the distance from now until next Wednesday was as an abyss not to be bridged, hardly to be endured. The days would pass, no doubt: "this time next week" would sooner or later come. I was philosopher enough always to support myself with this positive belief; but at the moment, after emergence from bliss, I felt that all one's doings, all one's comings and goings and eatings and sleepings and playings of games, all would be vanity and an ache or numb acquiescence, so much stretched-out patience in a void. One week I found out that if I went into the city and waited at the railway bookstall until the London train came in I could sometimes actually buy *The Boy's Friend* late on Tuesday evening, towards nine o'clock. After an eternity of suspense the man behind the bookstall would open a parcel, and there, behold and see! were the folds of the green paper; and I would run from the station in possession, almost before anybody else, of the secret of what happened to Ferrers Lord when it was discovered (last week) that the supply of oxygen had run out while they were all in the submarine at the bottom of the Pacific Ocean. But now and again the train would arrive with no bundle of the London papers on it, and I had to go away empty, the summer evening wasted, the Manchester streets desolate, miles of them to tread before I reached home.

In the course of years I graduated to literature proper. I joined a "Free Library," one of those many municipal institutions which smell of rubber matting, with a reading-room of stuffy mackintoshes on wet nights. To join the lending library it was necessary to fill in a form and get it signed by somebody on the register of householders in Manchester and district. I was obliged to go to much trouble to find a "guarantor," because my own family seldom stayed at one address long enough to become enrolled on the official list of rent and ratepayers. According to the vicissitudes of fortune they moved from house to house; it was called, in the vivid poetic imagery of the lower orders of the period, "flitting." The removal took place under cover of darkness, so that the furniture would not be revealed to the next-door neighbours. My grandmother spent the better part of the last few years of her life in, as she called it, "getting straight."

When at last I became entitled to use the Free Library I was never out of it at evenings. There was a boys' department, a room of hushed suppressed animation on the part of those of us who sat in it, poring ostensibly over *Chums* or *Westward Ho!* while we were faced or menaced by a large framed notice on the wall exhorting:

SILENCE!

We would suffer terrible inward convulsions when one of us goaded another to laughter, by referring him to some line in a book or to some picture. An official in a uniform, named Mr. Petty, would watch us, and after much trial to his tolerance would come and order us out of the library. We would depart in single file, Mr. Petty marshalling us before him; then as soon as we reached the entrance hall, where stood a huge globe of the world, we would emit terrific hoots and yelps of derision, taking advantage of the echoing powers of the vaulted roof, and one of us would send the globe whizzing round and round, before we leaped down the steps into the muddy street.

At other times Mr. Petty might stop us at the entrance and ask us to show our hands; he wished to assure himself that they were clean enough not to soil or pollute municipally-owned literature. We would show him our hands, palms downward, and he would wrench them round and discover the day's deposit of soil or grime. He would order us to go home and wash them, but to return home was usually out of the question; one would surely be asked to go on an errand or chop firewood or something, so we all went into a field, which had a top-dressing of clay. We would find a puddle and clean our hands by using the clay as soap. Purest whiteness was instantly achieved, satisfactory even to Mr. Petty's hygienic eye; we were permitted to go into the boys' reading-room after all. But the clay had by this time stiffened the finger joints considerably, so that to turn over a page was a sufficient prompting to further mirth and caricature, and, most likely, to another exasperated appearance of Mr. Petty, another ejection, and another whizzing round of the globe of the world.

I was nearly sixteen years old before I used the lending library and literature proper, and put childish things behind me. For long I tried to remain loyal to Maxwell Scott, Henry St. John and Sidney Drew. I looked up their names in *Who's Who*; and when I couldn't find them I did not think the less of these writers, but regarded *Who's Who* as an incomplete work of reference. I am not sure that the first novel I ever read, bound in stiff covers—i.e. an authentic book—wasn't called *Paul Kelver*, by Jerome K. Jerome of all men, the humorist of the clerks of the 1890's. This novel, entirely forgotten now, was about a boy whose parents were young and shabby-genteel, living in a hopeless London suburb. The father was a sentimental failure without prospects; the mother was helpless and a darling. There was a scene where the boy wakes in the night and overhears his father and mother discussing his future, in a fantasy of self-deception. " On the whole, my dear," says the father, "I think I'd prefer it to be Cambridge." It was this novel which first stirred in me an awareness to the significance of ordinary things and events; how they can come to have strange meanings if you feel them at more than their face value, so to say, and not just as isolated and utilitarian phenomena. Jerome describes the morning after the funeral of Paul's mother; Paul hears his father pottering about in the next room, and from the dismal street outside, misty on the winter morning, comes the familiar cry, " Milk-oh! Milk-oh!" This cadence touched me greatly, and I lived for weeks with Paul and his father. The long vistas of suburban Manchester at twilight, with their decaying semi-detached houses, all of which had seen better days, became excruciatingly poignant to me, with whispers in the gardens and the echoes of music played long ago. I wrote to Jerome K. Jerome telling him that I thought his novel was " literature "; and he replied to me with a characteristic huskiness of voice—" I am glad you liked little Paul," he wrote.

Then I found Dickens, after much tramping of streets from lending library to lending library. The attendants behind the counters, spinsters of severe countenance, with pince-nez never quite straight, would most times tartly say " None in," meaning that not one novel by Dickens remained on the shelves; all were out and being read. Often I was obliged to wait weeks. One night, after traversing several Manchester municipalities in vain search of *Copperfield* or *Chuzzlewit* or *Bleak House* or *Nickleby* or *Dombey and Son*, I wandered tired and disconsolate into a general news-room of one of these libraries, having been finally repulsed from the lending counter with an even more than usually acidulous ‘None in.” I sat down at a table and by chance picked up the *Athenæum*, and read an article in which I was informed that Dickens was no longer being read; taste apparently was at last appreciating the finer literary sensibility possessed by Thackeray. I was bewildered. If Dickens was “no longer being read,” why could I so seldom get one of his novels out of the municipal lending libraries? At the age of sixteen I did not realise that when a literary critic declares that nobody is reading a certain author he really means nobody in his own particular coterie is reading him.

Discovering Dickens is one of the few really important events that occur in mortal life, like first love, or hearing music for the first time with understanding ears, or finding out that wine is not as nasty as it tastes if your first sip is taken while you are too young, and that food is not just so many meals to be eaten for the sake of sustenance. I am still of the opinion that human beings can confidently be divided into two broad classes, those who have it in them from birth onwards to appreciate Dickens and those who haven't. The second group should be avoided as soon as detected. They are fit for plots and strategems or, to say the least, they are short of capacity for life. It is necessary, also, to be on one's guard against spurious readers of Dickens, those who prefer *Edwin Drood* to *Chuzzlewit* because it is more literary in technique and plot-structure and what not.

I read Dickens intact and nothing else for a whole year. Sometimes I read him in filthy volumes from the library when at length I could catch him " in," volumes with pages often holding some deposit of food, or permanently stamped with a wet teacup. Sometimes I read him in a volume of the new and hideous Harmsworth editions, a shilling each, the first books of which I made a library, with a small bookshelf nailed to the wall of my attic, two shelves only to begin with. I read Dickens in bed and at meals and in the streets. He made real life shadowy for me, unreal and tedious. After a day's work in an office, I would read him on the tramcar and sometimes become so absorbed that I would be carried far beyond my proper destination, miles beyond, but I did not care. It was scarcely a case of reading at all ; it was almost an experience of a world more alive and dimensional than this world, heightened and set free in every impulse of nature ; not subtle and abnormal impulses but such as even a more or less illiterate youth could at once share. I soon realised that the current criticism of Dickens was nonsense ; he did not make a caricature of people ; he simply let me see them more than life-size. David Copperfield so often behaved and thought as I behaved and thought that I frequently lost my own sense of identity in him. I did not of course rationalise my reading of early Dickens in this way ; but essentially this is how he affected me. Mrs. Nickleby was my own grandmother when she related a day's happening ; Betsy Prig was my grandmother as well—she too would stroke her legs in front of the fire, lifting up her skirts to do so. And I would sit at her feet and listen, and when she wandered beyond hope of recall from an interesting theme I would look far into the dying embers and see faces and islands and caves of gold.

But Dickens is not fully to be explored until late in one's years, though from the beginning he is the most real of story-tellers, almost a teller of fairy tales, or of old moralities deprived of the obviously didactic homilies. It is his genius for the creation of a populous world that makes him appeal to an enormous body of readers in every age, and his power to transform crude melodrama into credible yet fantastic life by setting it in places we have all been at some time or other; then mightiest of all his gifts, he endows his characters, a whole London census of them, with a freedom of the will that impels them here, there and everywhere in abounding confusion and irrelevance, taking the author himself with them, as well as the rest of us, so that he not less than his readers turns the pages over wondering what is going to happen next. The subtler qualities of Dickens, the abiding ones which hold us through all our days and years, in spite of his lack of a "criticism of life," were born of a unique liberating power of imagination which ranged riotously and changed familiar humans of the lower and middle classes into their gigantic and everlasting prototypes, all as though seen under the condition of eternity by God in His first creative gusto and knowledge of their potentialities. The great artist exhausts his material, drains out the last juice of his orange. Pecksniff is the complete humbug plus energy of delight of the creative imagination as it explores nature, plus also the roar of creative laughter at its own discoveries. And all the life in Dickens, every nook and cranny, is illuminated by gleams of the dark lantern of boyhood; satire of age is wedded to a naïve and willing suspension of unbelief; sophistication and observation are at home and active in a wonderland as distorted but actual as Lewis Carroll's, peopled by ogres as well as by Micawbers, by monsters grotesque as any dragon and by Sam Weller; a realm of fog and rain and London soot, of warehouses and wharves and mouldy offices with black boxes full of legal documents hideous and as unfit to be looked at as skeletons; a realm of sunlit highways leading to the heart of Kent; of cheerful inns and secret whispering stones and steps lapped by the Thames; of noonday reality and of dreams and nightmares and corners in dark bedrooms containing moving things terrible to infancy. The abiding Dickens is, like any other artist, amoral in his outlook on his own creations. He shapes his rogues with far more conviction than he shapes his heroes, certainly with more glee. It is when he emerges from his material bearing traces of all the rich and various dyes and stains, to make a conventional judgment suitable for family readers of his day—it is then that we have to sigh and turn a stack of pages. But I would not miss one of them when I was a novitiate. With dismay I would see that I was approaching the end of a volume and I would wonder how I could somehow "make it last."

Forty years ago, boys did not find it as easy as it is

nowadays to approach Dickens in the right way. Pre-Chesterton criticism of him presented Dickens austerely on the whole, almost lamenting his " vulgarities " but granted him grace and salvation as a social reformer. We were supposed to go through *Nickleby* with a sort of hue-and-cry, hounding on Squeers to retribution and justice. But when at last his villainy was exposed, and long before in fact, we found him " lovable." " Ah ! " sighed Mr. Squeers, in the irretrievable ruin of his career, " at the delightful village of Dotheboys near Greta Bridge, in Yorkshire, youth are boarded, clothed, booked, washed, furnished with pocket-money, provided with all necessaries, instructed in all languages living and dead, mathematics, orthography, geometry, astronomy, trigonometry—this is a altered state of trigonomics, this is ! A double l-all, everything, a cobbler's weapon. U-p—up adjective, not down. S-q-u-double e-r-s Squeers, noun substantive, educator of youth. Total, all up with Squeers." We must make our own soundings and chartings in the arts ; nobody can explore for us—which is all to the good, so that we may all one day climb to our own peak, silent in Darien. I alone, myself and unaided, discovered that Dickens was a great comic writer because with him humour is a consequence and not a starting-point ; that it comes almost unexpectedly from springs of character suddenly released. The modern comic-writer goes straight for the laugh and gets it by incongruity of circumstance and a trick of words. Dickens did not set himself deliberately to be comic ; he went within the skin of his people and became oblivious to the effects they make. He is Mrs. Gamp, so much so that he feels her anxiety about whether there is a " parapidge " outside the window of the sick-chamber, in case of fire. Such details of anxiety and concern do not come to the mind of merely inventive writers. Dickens' characters have a volition which takes them as though beyond the creator's control. Dickens wept when Little Paul died, and he laughed until tears came to his eyes when he overheard the conversation of Mrs. Gamp and Betsy Prig, and took it all down from a kind of dictation. He should be read with this same willing suspension of egotistical scepticism. Then he will lead you, as he led the boy that was once myself and as he has led a myriad of the chosen, to what Chesterton has called the Inn at the end of the world.

On a winter night, in my cold attic, with newspapers piled for warmth on my bed, in a garret-room uncarpeted, even without oilcloth, bare boards and sometimes the sound of a mouse gnawing away at one of them, a candle burning a small circle of flame in the gloom, I read for the first time the scene in *Pickwick* where Sam Weller composes a Valentine, and reads it to his father, while the old man stands with his back to the fire of the parlour of the Blue Boar. Sam, sitting in the box, pen in hand, dips it into the ink to be ready for any corrections, and begins to read :

> " ' Lovely . . .' "
>
> " Stop," said Mr. Weller, ringing the bell. " A double glass o' the inwariable, my dear."
>
> " Very well, sir," replied the girl ; who with great quickness appeared, vanished, returned, and disappeared.

"They seem to know your ways here," observed Sam.

"Yes," replied his father. "I've been here before, in my time. Go on, Sammy."

"'Lovely creetur,'" repeated Sam.

"Tain't in poetry, is it?" interposed his father.

"No, no," replied Sam.

"Wery glad to hear it," said Mr. Weller. "Poetry's unnat'ral; no man ever talked poetry 'cept a beadle on boxin'-day, or Warren's blackin', or Rowland's oil, or some of them low fellows; never you let yourself down to talk poetry, my boy. Begin agin, Sammy."

"'Lovely creetur i feel myself a dammed——'"

"That ain't proper," said Mr. Weller, taking his pipe from his mouth.

"No; it ain't 'dammed,'" observed Sam, holding the letter up to the light, "it's 'shamed,' there's a blot there—'I feel myself ashamed.'"

"Wery good," said Mr. Weller. "Go on."

"'Feel myself ashamed, and completely cir——' I forget what this here word is," said Sam, scratching his head with the pen, in vain attempts to remember.

"Why don't you look at it, then?" inquired Mr. Weller.

"So I *am* a-lookin' at it," replied Sam, "but there's another blot. Here's a 'c,' and a 'i,' and a 'd.'"

"Circumwented, p'raps," suggested Mr. Weller.

"No, it ain't that," said Sam, "'circumscribed'; that's it."

"That ain't as good a word as 'circumwented,' Sammy," said Mr. Weller gravely.

"Think not?" said Sam.

"Nothin' like it," replied his father.

"But don't you think it means more?" inquired Sam.

"Vell p'raps it's a more tenderer word," said Mr. Weller, after a few moments' reflection. "Go on, Sammy."

Such a scene is not invented; such conversation cannot be reproduced from the resources of the art of fiction proper; to talk of "circumscribed" as, in *any* circumstances, a more tenderer word would never have occurred to any great writer who was not more than a writer. None except the Wellers have felt the English language in that way.

Old Weller with the warmth of the fire on his back: I could feel it in my bed while the winter wind blew and set flapping a loose piece of brown paper stuck on a broken window-pane; Sam with his eyes screwed as he deciphered his own handwriting in an interior of cosiness, his father's pleated cape and the flavours of a double-glass of the "inwariable"—I read of these things deep into the night, and I heard snow fall with a thud from the roofs, and in the distance a clock struck one o'clock.

A boy's reading is honest; he has no axe of culture or literary appreciation to grind, especially if like myself and Dickens too, he suffers from a "defective education." I tried in vain for a long time to live in Thackeray with my imagination as well as read him with a developing understanding of the craft of fiction. But his books remained for me strictly books written by an accomplished author. To this day I should, if pressed, and for all my relish of Thackeray as a man of his world, and for all my love of Beatrix Esmond, call him a prosaic genius and not, as Dickens was, a poetic genius; less creative, less a weaver of spells that enchant and enhance reality. I can account for Thackeray in terms of the evolution of the English novel. Dickens was spontaneously generated, and fabulous, and never to be repeated.

Somehow I never fell under the sway of Scott; to this day I have not read a novel by him—my loss, of course, but as C. E. Montague once said to me, you can't begin to read Scott late in life. Even Stevenson failed to grip me, entirely, though I stayed in bed all one Sunday reading *Treasure Island*, as I shall tell again later —while my trousers were being mended and cleaned. From Dickens I went at a tangent to Hardy, and here again a boy's instincts were reliable. Meredith at this time was set against Hardy much as Thackeray against Dickens, as the finer literary artist, the subtler mind, more alive to a civilised view of men and women. The contemporary neglect of Meredith is deplorable but not to be surprised at in an ignobly sentimental and brutal age governed by Demos; in some of his poetry we can hear the most poignantly tragic overtones of any written since Shakespeare:

Love, that had robbed us of immortal things
This little moment mercifully gave,
Where I have seen across the twilight wave
The swan sail with her young beneath her wings.

But novels cannot be revealed in flashes of wit and imagination; the characters and the places must be seen "in the round" and dimensional; this naïve view of the essence of the novelist's art holds as true nowadays as it did when Cervantes said that every novel should begin with somebody setting out on a journey. As though unfolded in a slow changing sunset, Hardy's universe became for me, and has remained, a part of what might be called my picture of life, not in contrast but complementary to the one revealed by the humanists and the laughers. For months I read him and nobody else; all our introductions to the masters should be as a plunge into one immense engulfing sea. For months I was as the spy watching at a lonely cross-road where a man stood, undecided which way to turn; if he went one way instead of the other the whole of his destiny would be altered.

When I read Hardy in my seventeenth year, his philosophy, his pessimism and the rest of it, meant as little to me as the long arm of his coincidences. He was all pictures and presence—people in arrested fateful attitudes, a frieze of the fields and heaths, and lanes and barns and the pavements of country towns. The reddleman playing cards by the light of a glow-worm; the sword of Sergeant Troy; the weary trail of Fanny along the roadway supporting her will-power by imagining that the next milestone was her destination; Tess toiling in the heat of the vale; the leit-motif of the pig's guts striking Jude on the face; the plash of the pebble in the pool as Eustacia Vye waited in the darkness of the night; the indifference of Egdon Heath, and the endless growth and dissolution of all the earthly particles, while the pitiful story is told of those who live there for a moment.

It is from imagination and not from ideas or a "body of thought" that the power comes which makes a book live with us all our lives, from youth to the chimney-corner of age. This is a platitude of the sort I used to underline in my more serious reading as a boy; I would make a note in the margin—"Very good," or "I agree." A boy does not regard his books as part of culture; at least, boys of forty years ago didn't. We went into them neck-high for fun and illusion. We did not distinguish between our authors and the way they transmuted their material. In later life, no doubt, the critical attitude to literature brings pleasures of a refined æsthetic order. But I doubt if they console for that lost first willing surrender to the author's most simple and direct invocation—that is to say, if we are so unfortunate as to lose it at all. Give me the old hypnotic gesture and I can still succumb, and go through the silent watches of the night held by the old spell, reading just another page before turning out the light, sometimes even glancing ahead a chapter or two to find out, or to get just an inkling, of what happened in the end, even as in a world so remote that I cannot easily believe I once lived in it, I ached and ached for next week's thrilling instalment in one of the "ripping" narratives in *The Boy's Friend* by Henry St. John.

It was a great day in my life when the Public Library opened its shelves to the public, one and all. So far we had been obliged to appear before a counter and solicit the spinsters for our literature. I could seldom guess whether or not they approved of one's selections from the catalogue, though I detected a certain if momentary glare of doubt through a pince-nez when, not yet a grown man, I asked for *Jude the Obscure.*

So, at the age a boy goes into long trousers—one of life's periods of irretrievable separation from all that has gone before—I found myself for the first time really amongst books, bound books, rows and terraces of them reaching upwards, so that I had to stretch myself to see the titles and the author's names. The shelves were arranged in sections, alphabetically, thus: *Accountancy*, *Agriculture*, and so on to *Zoology* and *Zoroastrianism*. The room was gloomy; the atmosphere heavy with that penal silence peculiar to public libraries. I tried as far as possible to inspect the shelves at those times of the day or the evening when few folk would be about. Often I was there almost alone, peering high and low. Soon I came to remember the position of almost every book, able to detect at sight whether it was "in" or "out." There they stood, rank on rank, new and old, shiny and shabby, all erect except one or two aslant or tumbled over for lack of adjacent support, all patiently waiting, some with constant readers and friends, others neglected.

I cannot account for it, but I seldom chose a second-rate book, even in these early years of my reading. My formal education had been worse than none at all, obtained at the Board school round the corner. I knew next to nothing of anything. One year I was engrossed in *The Boy's Friend*, a little later in Dickens and Mark Twain and Jerome K. Jerome. Then, without scarcely a bridge-passage, I was deep in the authors who to this day I regard the best discovered in a life-time. I knew no music to speak of except Sullivan and

Leslie Stuart and "When Other Lips," out of *The Bohemian Girl.* I had seen Shakespeare acted vividly, but badly I suppose, by touring companies dominated by Osmond Tearle; but I had not read a word of him. I had not ventured beyond arithmetic into the authentic world of mathematics; and my conception of science ended with a vision of Watt watching a kettle on the boil. None the less in this same benighted if gestatory state I became a bookworm, living for books, waking early on the frozen mornings to get through a few pages before going out to work in office or factory; reading in the street whenever and wherever I happened to be walking as an errand boy; even at nightfall running from lamp-post to lamp-post; reading books at meals, not knowing what food I ate; then after the long day's durance in a city that bought in the cheapest and sold in the dearest markets, a scurry to the library before closing time, followed by, and best of all, the silence and absorption of my bedroom, the enchantment before sleep, with sometimes a shock caused by the thud of the book on the floor, waking me after I had apparently been reading one and the same line for hours.

Most readers know how, when they are looking in a book for a certain passage and it eludes them, they can remember on which part of a page the passage occurs, whether at the bottom or the top, whether on the page at the right or the left. It is possibly not so common to remember the exact place and circumstances in which we first came upon a passage that has remained in our minds ever afterwards. If I were lying on my deathbed, with only an hour left to think for the last time on all my remembered pleasures, I would recall the evening when I stood in a queue outside the Prince's Theatre in Manchester, waiting for the " shilling-pit " to open for some play or other, and I was reading " Pippa Passes." My position in the queue was directly outside the window of Dingley's flower shop (one of the first to advertise " Say it with flowers "), a window from which colour and warmth and fragrance shone into the chill of a foggy night. Suddenly these lines started from the pages of my book, which I was holding with bitterly cold fingers, and pierced my imagination so that I could not read further, but caught my breath and forgot where I was, as I saw the pitiful Sebald and Otima hiding in the night:

Buried in the woods we lay, you recollect;
Swift ran the searching tempest overhead;
And ever and anon some bright white shaft
Burned thro' the pine-tree roof, here burned and there,
As if God's messenger thro' the close wood screen
Plunged and replunged his weapon at a venture
Feeling for guilty thee and me. . . .

Forked lightning a sword, " plunged at a venture "— the metaphor blinded me with its flash of drama and awe; there are few such metaphors in all poetry.

To some people a strain of music or a pressed leaf found in an album, or a particular scent, brings back to memory an old place or emotion. For myself a sentence or period in an old book is more potent and murmurous in the mind even than a bundle of half-forgotten but suddenly unearthed love letters. It is as though I were able to recall the first days on which I could breathe, or taste, or see; for I truly believe that a great book read for the first time, at the right impressionable moment, is in the most solemn meaning of the word a revelation. If we read well, with imagination, each book increases the antennæ, the cat's whiskers, by which we come to feel and extend consciousness and squeeze through just opened physical doors and apertures into the spaces of heightened vibratory life.

Again, the scene of my attic recurs, in the dead of night, as ever. The candle now steady, now faltering; the clothes drawn as closely over my shoulders as I can get them, and only the tips of my fingers exposed to the cold as I hold the book which this time is *The Woodlanders* by Thomas Hardy, and I come to the end of the story, the last paragraph, the requiem of Mart South:

" Now, my own own love," she whispered, " you are mine, and on'y mine; for she forgot 'ee at last, although for her you died. But I—whenever I get up I'll think of 'ee, and whenever I lie down I'll think of 'ee again. Whenever I plant the young larches I'll think that none can plant as you planted; and whenever I split a gad, and whenever I turn the cider wring, I'll say none could do it like you. If I ever forget your name let me forget home and heaven . . . But no, no, my love, I can never forget 'ee; for you was a good man, and did good things."

After I read the last sentence, I put down the book, blew out the candle—the smell of smouldering wick!—and I buried my head in my pillow, and for the first of many times in my fifty-odd years, I wept—not from sorrow or sentiment, but from actual contact with the complex texture of human nature; how it can, without knowing it until the great artist discloses it, achieve nobleness in small natural things.

Once I was pushing a handcart along a Manchester street, working as a handyman (*aetat* 18) for a joiner and builder known as Ed. Moss on his bill-heads; on this occasion I was delivering some long planks of wood to what was technically known as a "job." I directed the handcart by steering one end of a plank; the handcart itself was rather out of touch with me; and I would from time to time pause and come to a standstill, and, using the plank as a reading desk, get through at least one more page. It was this way I experienced one of the shocks to be received in classic fiction—in *Tom Jones* in the chapter entitled a "very long chapter containing a very great incident."

Since I discovered *Tom Jones* nearly forty years ago I have read it every other year, every word (except the interpolated story about "The Man on the Hill"). Sophia Western was my first love among heroines of fiction, and to this day there is none like her, but I see her always through the humorous eyes of her creator, adored by him in one sentence, the most tender and playful and pathetic in all the language and range of the English novel:

"Come my bright love of fame, inspire my glowing breast; not thee I call, who, over swelling tides of blood and tears, dost bear our hero on to glory, while sighs of millions waft his spreading sails; but thee, fair, gentle maid, whom Mnesis, happy nymph, first on the banks of Hebrus did produce. Thee, whom Maeonia educated, whom Mantua charmed, and who, on that fair hill which overlooks the proud metropolis of Britain, sat'st, with thy Milton, sweetly tuning the heroic lyre; fill my ravished fancy with the hopes of charming ages yet to come. Foretell me that some tender maid, whose grandmother is yet unborn, hereafter, when under the fictitious name of Sophia, she reads the real worth which once existed in my Charlotte, shall from her sympathetic breast send forth the heaving sigh. So thou teach me not only to foresee, but to enjoy, nay even to feed on future praise. Comfort me by a solemn assurance, that when the little parlour in which I sit at this instant shall be reduced to a worse furnished box, I shall be read with honour by those who never knew nor saw me, and whom I shall neither know nor see."

Few of the heroines of fiction would I wish to desire and love in real life. Becky Sharp I might sit with at dinner now and again and afterwards enjoy some sport or dalliance; but I'd keep my distance. Sometimes a sultry vision or presence comes back to me when I think of some of Conrad's women; and when I was adolescent the women in Meredith swept me off my feet; nowadays I see them all as somewhat fabulous, fit for figureheads on the prows of ships. Eustacia Vye has attracted me with her dark slow-fires of tragic passion; but with women I am all for a quiet life. Hardy's women are fraught with disturbance; all except the sweet girl Thomasin, my next love after Sophia. I am not forgetting Beatrix Esmond, whom I worshipped as a matter of course until, not long ago, I re-read the celebrated description of her descent of the staircase:

"She was a brown beauty; that is, her eyes, hair and eyebrows and eyelashes were dark; her hair curling with rich undulations, and waving over her shoulders; but her complexion was as dazzling white as snow in sunshine; except her cheeks, which were a bright red, and her lips, which were of a still deeper crimson. Her mouth and chin, they said were too large and full, and so they might be for a goddess in marble, but not for a woman whose eyes were fire, whose look was love, whose voice was the sweetest low song, whose shape was perfect symmetry, health, decision, activity, whose foot as it planted the ground was firm but flexible, and whose motion, whether rapid or slow, was always perfect grace—agile as a nymph, lofty as a queen—now melting, now imperious, now sarcastic—there was no single movement of hers but was beautiful. As he thinks of her, he who writes feels young again, and remembers a paragon. . . ."

Lovely, or rather sumptuous!—a period decoration. I wish Thackeray had left it at "As he thinks of her, he who writes feels young again." Better still if he had called her no more than a "brown beauty."

But I am sorry that novelists no longer give us their asides and comments. By the latest decrees "our author" may scarcely set foot in the house of his own novel; the reader must not be allowed to suspect his presence. The idea nowadays is to suggest that anybody in the world is telling the story except "our author." The illusion of objective reality must be obtained at all costs; the story must be treated or looked at from "successive aspects"—from a detached point of view Conrad tells his tale through the medium of Lord Jim; but even this obliquity of narrative doesn't go far enough, for Lord Jim is merely usurping the author's total knowledge; he knows how everything began and how it all will end. So Henry James causes the significances and action of *The Ambassadors* to pass first through the mind of one of his characters *before* these significances and action have reached the reader. The man Strether, as he is actually *in* the story while it is happening, can have no prevision of consequences; what's to come is for him still unsure. A masterpiece of technique and sensibility and finely shaded prose, each sentence a vibration of subtle awareness—but, oh, how tired we become of Strether! I am not presuming to lodge an objection to James's method or to Conrad's. This is a book of personal tastes, and I express them ready to admit that occasionally they may go contrary to acquired æsthetic and theory. I hope that at no point do I show an impatience with or reaction against any artist, without conveying at the same time a respect for his genius. The present age in general does not read Henry James; possibly there is no leisure for a writer who so far from endeavouring to simplify language and thought goes willingly into devious but pregnant ways of consciousness, subtilising to more and more impalpable contours and shades the canvas of his novel; "the lovely art of foreshortening," as James himself called it —"the refinement and ecstasies of method." Not far from the spot in which I wrote this passage stands a public library, a noble edifice fronting one of the most beautiful natural sights in the world, the harbour of Sydney. In one of the alcoves where the volumes repose, sometimes touched with the Pacific sunlight coming through stained-glass windows, the beautiful New York collected edition of Henry James may be seen, the embalmed posterity of a writer whose shade, if ever it wanders as far from Rye as this, will press an ironic lip, open his eyes a little wider, and by oblique polite dumb-show (in a place where silence is golden) express his approval that most of the pages are still uncut. As I look at these pale-green volumes I marvel at the content of them, the patience of each sentence, the inwardness of mind and imagination; this world of quiet searchings, and implications—" a world worthy of his own master faculty, in which human beings, when confronted, saw mysteries in one another's gestures, and profundities in their words, and took joy in each other's insight, like brave antagonists in each other's strength, a world in which they could exclaim about one another that they were 'wonderful' and 'beautiful', where they belonged to, or fought with each other, on levels of intimacy which had never been described before."

The quotation is from Desmond MacCarthy's essay on Henry James; he also writes of James this sentence, the most pathetically beautiful tribute in an age of lost elegancies, subtleties, and courteous ironic attitudes: " He was horrified by the brutality and rushing confusion of the world, where the dead are forgotten, old ties cynically snapped, old associations disregarded, where one generation tramples down the other, where the passions are blind, and men and women are satisfied with loves and friendships which are short, common and empty. I picture him as flying with frightened eyes and stopped ears from that City of Destruction, till the terrified bang of his sanctuary door leaves him palpitating but safe ; free to create a world which he could people with beings who had leisure and the finest faculties for comprehending and appreciating each other, where the reward of goodness was the recognition of its beauty, and where the past was not forgotten."

" Where the past was not forgotten " ; this is a cry from the heart of those of us who in our youth felt a quickened idealism as we read Meredith, and the stirring of a strange emotion—known later to be compassion—as we read Hardy, and a dawning of the sense of Time's indifference, of its delicately-woven texture of years, so easily snapped, as we read (with labour and conceit) Henry James. He is the author for experience and age, and for those sensibilities that have been hurt by cruelties unconsciously dealt, cruelties made almost lovable or beautiful by ironic reminiscence. But when I was not yet twenty, how could I forgive him for what he wrote of Arnold Bennett and H. G. Wells and others who were making novels out of our own drab and shapeless years and struggles—Mr. Polly and Kipps and Uncle Ponderevo ? " There is to my vision, no authentic, and no really interesting and no *beautiful*, report of things on the novelist's part unless a particular detachment has operated, unless the great stewpot or crucible of the imagination, of the observant and recording and interpreting mind in short, has intervened and played its part—and this detachment, this chemical transmutation for the æsthetic, the representational, end is terribly wanting in autobiography brought, as the horrible phrase is, up to date." So wrote James, and I hated him for it!

Detachment and an intervening impersonal æsthetic and form—yes, these are constant joys when we are above the battle, connoisseurs of life and literature. There is room for all sorts surely, except vulgarity. I for one have still my moments when I prefer that a novelist should not remain always detached, like a god who, having set into motion his world, is now unable to change its course. I love a show of omniscience, of freedom of action and liberty for an author to dote, if he wish, on his own handiwork, or to make a friendly approach to his readers and to play with them—as Fielding plays with us when he lets us into a secret in *Tom Jones* (out of sheer necessity of plot)—a secret "which we have had no proper opportunity to reveal before." Nobody wishes to be winked at and ogled by the novelist; and Thackeray's moralising becomes at times tedious. The artist likes to conceal that he is tied to his medium; he does not wish always to reveal the hand subdued to what it works in. He is like the fond parent performing conjuring tricks at a Christmas party; as he tries to create the illusion of reality he, in effect, shows us his empty palms and says "I have nothing up my sleeve." If he is a disciple of Henry James—as we have seen—he conceals it up the sleeve of Strether.

The oblique method has nothing in it that is commendable *a priori*. "Grau, grau, ist alle Theorie"—the main thing is the genius employing it, and the nature of the material. Obviously a Flaubert must not butt-in upon the provincial scene of Madame Bovary. But the contemporary fashion has insisted on a total ban on the novelist's slightest claim to prerogative of personal ownership. When was written the last great novel in the first person, or instance? What would the higher criticism say if Howard Spring towards the conclusion of *Fame is the Spur* (nearly a *great* novel) had called on the Muses—" Come, all of these, and more, if possible; for arduous is the task I have undertaken; and without all your assistance, will I find, be too heavy for me to support." Such an invocation in a modern story would be an affectation; but may we not be charmed occasionally by an equivalent and modern playfulness? Where the theme is tragic there is of course no room for an " aside "; Hardy's famous banality at the conclusion of *Tess* is a classic warning against an author revealing and committing himself out of turn.

When I was very young, I wrote a novel myself, and one of the characters was a millionaire (probably a relation of Ferrers Lord); and he was supposed to live in a most sumptuous mansion and to be very cultured and a brilliant conversationalist, from whose lips epigrams of quicksilver flashed at every sentence. But when it came to getting on to paper all this splendour and culture and wit, I was rather at a loss. I had never actually seen an opulent mansion, and there were no cinemas to help me in those days. As for the conversation of my hero, I confess I couldn't think of anything learned or dazzling enough to put into his mouth. So I took refuge in the omniscient " aside "; I gave my word for it to my readers that he " held the listeners spellbound, by the profundity of his ideas and the lambent flame of his irony."

I am waiting for another novel in which the author will range where he will, entering the mind of this character and that, yet retaining his own identity and encircling the earth on the wings of his imagination; for if a creator may not know all, and see ends in beginnings, who indeed may? The next great writer of fiction, I believe, will return to the ancient faith; he will accept the responsibility of godhead, and he will be conscious, as he writes "Chapter I" at the head of the first page of his manuscript, that he is uttering a *Fiat Lux*.

I must confess, though, that when I began my experiments in reading, I sometimes resented the old authors' liberty to go here and there in their tales, without giving due warning. I was shocked to dismay and helpless suspense, on my first enchantments in *Chuzzlewit*, when I came to the end of chapter twenty, after Tom Pinch has told Pecksniff that old Mr. Chuzzlewit is on the way to his house:

> "Dear, dear!" cried Tom, "what have I done? I hoped it would be a pleasant surprise, sir. I thought you would like to know."
>
> But at that moment a loud knocking was heard at the hall door.

What a situation! Turning breathless the page for the next chapter I suffered the torment and frustration endured by thousands surely. For this is what I read: "Chapter Twenty-One . . . The knocking at Mr.

Pecksniff's door, though loud enough, bore no resemblance whatever to the noise of an American railway train at full speed. . . ." Mr. Pecksniff's house is more than a thousand leagues away. Dickens has for a while left us in the air. It was hard not to turn whole chapters over to pick up the broken thread; but marvellously did Dickens at once lure us along another way; in a flash he had us in thrall again, plunged into the New World with Mr. La Fayette Kettle, editor of the *Watertoast Gazette*, and General Choke:

> " 'Upon my word,' cried Martin, laughing, 'since you do me the honour to consider me his' (The British Lion's) 'representative, I have only to say that I never heard of Queen Victoria reading the What's-his-name Gazette, and that I scarcely think it probable.' "
>
> General Choke smiled upon the rest, and said, in patient and benignant explanation:
>
> " 'It is sent to her, sir. It is sent to her. Per mail.' "

But I am spending too much time remembering fiction in my early books. Frankly I soon became indulgent about novels. I did not include them—not even those by Tolstoy and Meredith—in my Schema of reading. My grandfather, who surprisingly would reveal a distant connection with literature—he belonged to a Mechanics Institution round about 1865—once picked up *Anna Karenina*, fresh if slightly soiled from the public library, and having inspected it at extreme arm's length, said, "What are you doing with this trash? Read proper books, young man—*proper* books." He did not mean books that were not improper; he had in mind books of strict intellectual, even philosophical content.

And one day I found one of the most far-reaching discoveries of my life. How many books do we read in a lifetime of which we can say that they open doors in our consciousness, that after reading them we are different, and that even as we turn over the pages we feel sight coming where there has been no sight? Such a book I picked up from a deserted shelf in the public library one darkening afternoon. It was old-fashioned in appearance, with marbled binding, and inside was an inscription: "Presented to the Manchester Corporation Libraries by Seth Oldacre, 1888." This volume was none other than *A Biographical History of Philosophy: From Thales to Comte*, by George Henry Lewes. I had never heard of George Henry Lewes, and my idea of a philosopher was a man who tolerated toothache patiently and didn't allow troubles to get him down easily. A shop in Manchester, very stately and aloof, had a sign announcing, "Makers of Philosophical Instruments"; and I puzzled my brains wondering how a compass or a slide-rule could be said to be philosophical. I was as innocent as the driven snow of what Lewes was writing about when I opened his history and began to read.

I have not seen this history for nearly half a century; I have not in that time heard a mention of it. No doubt it is hopelessly out of date, with its nineteenth-century rationalistic bias and static psychology. But I doubt if a better book of its kind has been presented to the layman. Lewes was a fine writer on actors and plays, and he brought to his history an acute dramatic sense of the endless quest of the metaphysicians down the ages, and of the clash of dialectic. He was not the abstract professor, aloof and merely academic; irony emerges as he demonstrates the elaborate logic of this and that system, cloud-capped palaces of idealism, and bastions of realism sturdily built on the sure earth, all of them in turn discredited, "dispossessed, chuck'd down." The vain prevision of induction; the equally vain reservations of deduction; the unwearying search for the thing-in-itself—it was as thrilling as a detective story told in Lewes's quick etchings of exposition. To realise what has never been suspected before—that things may be known beyond doubt to the senses yet there is some doubt whether they really exist as we perceive and feel them!—little in all our lives as *experiencing* beings can compare with this birth of awareness to metaphysical significances and values. I firmly believe that the man who has not, even in a superficial way, received some instruction in metaphysics; who has not considered the problems of how we know and what is, or may be, knowledge; who has not contemplated the distinction between perception and conception, between objects and the mind that makes intelligent order out of objects—such a man remains a child during all the length of his days. The familiar complaint against metaphysics is that it is a study that gets you nowhere, can settle nothing and is powerless to arrive at demonstrable truths. But it is because metaphysics is not limited by the workings of the practical understanding that it *is* the "divine" study—pure thought exercised for the sake of pure thought, and, like art, of no material value.

We have lately had enough of thought directed by practical reason, which means scientific thought; the atomic bomb is a truth of a kind not in the power of metaphysics to demonstrate. The truths of metaphysics are, like the truths of music, intuitive and not mutually exclusive; on the contrary they are complementary. The only falsity in metaphysics is a logical flaw or dissonance within a given system. Pure metaphysics does not in fact postulate human beings and their "rights" and "wrongs" at all; it is a study which the gods would have cultivated just the same if there had never been a terrestrial universe.

When I ran into Lewes, I was one of G. W. Foote's youthful followers, an avowed atheist, though even to myself I dared not say the word. I compromised with "agnostic." I read *The Freethinker* but never in public, usually at home in the lavatory. But Foote was not exactly metaphysical; he emulated Colonel Ingersoll and Bradlaugh, and I have myself heard him repeat Bradlaugh's notorious challenge to God to strike him dead on a public platform if He really existed; he (Mr. Foote) would give Him (God) five minutes. And there Mr. Foote stood, watch in hand, timing Him, while we sat and waited. I had not suspected that there was any doubt about the demonstrable reality of the external universe during my early advocacy of blasphemy and scepticism; the atom was the corner stone of the universe, palpable as any stone in the street. If I had been told that Bishop Berkeley had argued that matter did not exist I might have followed Dr. Johnson's example and kicked the stone away, saying, "I refute him thus."

So, after a few days and nights of Lewes, I found myself, like Kant, aroused from dogmatic slumbers. Suppose I *had* kicked the stone? What should I have known of it as a thing demonstrably existent outside my mind? Suppose I had been born sightless and lacking sense of touch? I should then scarcely have known I was even kicking; as for the stone I could not have come into contact with it at all. An unseen stone which I could not feel! Was it likely, the uninstructed but fascinated young metaphysician asked himself, that in the struggle of evolution the human race had acquired exactly the senses necessary fully to comprehend the external universe? Sights and sounds and smells and taste and hardness and softness are sensations, not facts of reality. If I could believe in an Omniscient Creator it would be enough to say that He had endowed us with just the right keys of sense whereby every door in the house of objective truth might be opened. "Thou hast made known to me the ways of life," as St. Peter assures us. But I was not a believer. So I seized on the "primary" qualities of Locke, as supports for my materialism. Colour, sound, warmth, taste, solidity: these are "secondary" qualities, because the object cannot be proved to possess them. But size, motion, number and extension are surely real. Something certainly exists outside of us in time and space, even if our senses make an arbitrary picture of this Something, even if it is just a heap of matter without colour, warmth, taste, odour. A blue sky might be only a sensation of sight, but there's no actual way of proving that a blue sky is not really there. If the fire was not in itself hot, at least it was capable of conveying a message to the senses; and it was indeed *I* who felt the burn as I picked up the hot cinder.

Then Bishop Berkeley came forward and he asked—almost quizzing me personally from the pages of Lewes—have we grounds for conceiving a "reality" outside of our minds corresponding in the slightest to our ideas of it? All knowledge is perception; the essence of an object is that it is perceived. We can know nothing but our mental reactions. The materialists denied the validity of the "secondary" qualities of reality—warmth, colour, taste and so on. So, begorrah, by the same token, the "primary" qualities are also rendered invalid to logic. We cannot go outside of mind; we can have no link or nexus with an external universe of any kind metaphysically conceivable. We know only mind. And as nothing can exist without being perceived, this "world" of ours, and all that lives, moves and has being therein, is an idea in the mind of God. He is Reality, the only Existence! Can't you see the Manchester youth, in free libraries, tramcars, under the street lamps and in his midnight attic, groping his way through Lewes and changing the dry-minded lover of George Eliot into the most exciting writer of detective tales?

I cannot pretend that these conclusions of Berkeley caused me to lose a single night's sleep. I was only the more enchanted when I came to David Hume and his chessboard move which captured a Bishop. I went about my day's work, much as David Hume himself, on the assumption that chairs were indeed solid and substantial enough to be sat on, and that a burn was not safely to be thought of as one of my private sensations but might conceivably reside in the public fire outside me, and that the sun would certainly rise in the east to-morrow, if only from habit. I derived much joy from the thought that W. G. Foote was an atheist in the mind of God. Metaphysics was fun. Yet without my own awareness of it, I was going through the best training that metaphysics can give; I was experiencing that uncertainty which helps to discourage the cock-sureness of adolescent brains. I was discovering that logic is not truth.

The chessboard of metaphysics, the ironic moves on it! Kant corners both Berkeley and Hume in one or two moves. For though Kant was unable to go beyond appearance to reality, and though his metaphysic ended at an attempt to show us how we might know rather than what we actually do know, he at least spared us from a conception of mind as a passive uncreative blank tablet—a sort of blotting-paper of consciousness upon which the external universe doodles away endlessly and without meaning. Knowledge is not all accumulated sense-data. Mind is not a passive mirror of the external world; or a sort of camera obscura. It is not Berkeley's closed-in chamber of self-existent mind, perceived only by God, without beginning and end. It is not David Hume's scepticism either. Mind is creative; it gives shape to sense-experience. A clock strikes; the mind does not take in each sound as an isolated phenomena; it adds them up. The mind possesses creative power, using innate instruments or "categories" by means of which the never-ceasing inrush of sensations are put into significant form, integrated into knowledge and intelligence.

But denouement in metaphysics as drama occurred for me when I read Schopenhauer. I have frankly not, as Mr. Boffin might say, been slap bang through the moderns—Alexander, Whitehead and the rest. I have come to read metaphysics now as a form of art; and for that reason I can always return to Schopenhauer, the only writer of metaphysics with grandeur of imagination. The Kantian Thing-in-Itself is changed by Schopenhauer into devouring Will; the only reality—a blind will to live. We can feel our bondage to it in all that we do; all our senses and nerves, every function of being, are a manifestation of appetite, a hungry urge on and on, ceaselessly. "The will is independent of knowledge and works blindly as in unconscious nature. It is the cause of war and the end of peace; the basis of what is serious, and the aim of the just; the inexhaustible source of wit, the key of all illusions and the meaning of all mysterious hints. We see it at every moment seat itself, as the true and hereditary lord of the world, out of the fullness of its own strength, upon the throne, and looking down thence with scornful glance, laugh at the preparations made to bind it, or imprison it, or at least to limit it and, whenever possible, keep it concealed, and even so to master it that it shall only appear as a subordinate, secondary concern of life."

The will is changeless. The true philosophy of history, says Schopenhauer, lies in the perception that, in all the endless motley complex of events, it is the self-same irrational being that is before us, which to-day pursues the same ends as it did yesterday. The will is oblivious to the individual. As Thing-in-Itself the will goes on creating only to destroy again. There is one way of escape for us—æsthetic imagination. In contemplation the will is quietened; we are freed from self. The ego is merged in the contemplation of art into a dream-world where there is no time and no space and therefore no opportunity for active will. In the blessedness of will-less perception, we may find peace. For the less the will is excited the less we suffer. In absorbing ourselves into beauty we can find the greatest wisdom; we are lifted beyond self and desire.

Depressing? It is an irrelevant objection in a metaphysical discussion. Must the world, which, as we have agreed—or haven't we?—may not exist, be pampered at every turn, picked up when it stumbles, petted when it cries in the dark, told to be good and then all is sure to come right in the end? Assurance of a personal immortality? I am reminded when people go about searching and praying for life after death of the general in Frederick the Great's army; his troops wavered before a withering fire, so he leaped ahead, sword aloft, and rallied them by shouting, "Come on, you cowards—what's the matter with you? Do you all want to live for ever?" To conquer fear of death is not difficult as a man grows older; much more difficult is it to conquer fear of life. A pessimist has been described as a man who spent a week-end with an optimist. In an age of brisk science, with our leaders of thought and politics still mumbling the old incantations to the various and variable tribal gods, it is a refreshment of mind, even of spirit, to luxuriate once in a while in the pessimism of Schopenhauer. A tragic metaphysic lends dignity to life; it is a paltry notion that God as First Cause is even aware of, let alone interested in, a phenomenal universe; and that humans cannot fend for themselves during a brief day of sun and frost but must have heavenly guidance in times of war or peace. That there is a dualism in our notions of nature and reality, an antinomy, is as self-evident a truth as "Cogito ergo sum." We can feel in ourselves the pulsations of evil as well as of good, no matter how chastened by thought or breeding. We neutralise them when the ego is absorbed in a higher and more universal self in which desire becomes only a gesture in a representation of the world, seen and realised æsthetically. Thus the artist may well be merely a shoemaker, shaping his material for love, lost to the materialist ends of his job. I believe in Good and Evil, a dualism which may or may not have had a beginning and may or may not come to an end. The dualism may indeed possess no meaning at all, considered *sub specie æternitatis*. The battle is here and now. Good is a matter of ways of life that increase the imagination and the understanding. Evil is ignorance that such ways can even exist; evil is uneducated reflex action. The battle would be spoiled and belittled for me and shorn of its grandeur, if I thought of the end as a thing arranged and foreseen in powerful mind of an Arch-Planner. I like to feel an ironic significance in the passing theatre of existence. The will-to-live as possible devil!—and first we must, like Perseus, look at the gorgon in the mirror, the mirror of the arts. Thomas Hardy ends *The Dynasts* with

> " *That the rages*
> *of the ages*
> *Shall be cancelled, and deliverance offered from the darts that were,*
> *Consciousness the Will informing till It fashion all things fair. . . .*"

Æsthetic consciousness alone can " fashion all things fair." It is the eye and ears, the senses and mind, of the spirit. But metaphysics is not a didactic torch lit to show poor humanity a way out of darkness and confusion ; its gleams are as a rainbow arched across the sky of thought, the refracted colour of all the mutations in the minds of thinkers who often talked poetry without knowing it.

Myself I have never, in spite of the luck of learning the A B C from Lewes at an early age, educated myself into trained metaphysics. But I have not perhaps fallen from grace in the eyes of the shades of the great system-builders whose works I have tried to fathom in my own way. I have not been content to serve metaphysics academically ; I have turned to them, as the metaphysicians would surely wish a novice to turn, in those moments when the external and palpable universe has made its most urgent and distracting claims. As I write this chapter, I hear outside my window sounds of revelry ; the world is celebrating another stage or milestone in its will-driven course ; does it really exist, this external world? The boy who more than thirty-five years ago discovered Lewes in a deserted shelf of a public library in Manchester was the father of the man trying to put down on paper, in times that are as distracting and troublous as usual, a far from clearly reasoned but deeply-felt view of the beauty and use of metaphysics as art and a guide to living, and as a remembered pleasure.

·IV·

I CANNOT remember how I became interested in cricket. There were no games organised at the Board school which I attended more or less irregularly, morning and afternoon, from the age of eight to thirteen, when I joined the ranks of the employed. These five years of my formal education were interrupted by an illness which kept me in bed nearly a year, suffering from what was at the time rather unscientifically known as an abscess on the lungs. A steam kettle maintained the temperature of my bedroom, and every morning the doctor, a clean polished gentleman with a black coat and striped trousers and a white border in his waistcoat, put some tubes to my chest, and listened. I liked the smell of him, the way he would flop his gloves into his tall hat.

The Board school did not extend its curriculum beyond the " three R's," a list of " dates " in English history, and some geography about peninsulas being nearly surrounded by water. The main thing apparently was to awaken us to a sense of inborn sin ; we were taught Scripture every morning at nine o'clock, and the boy who showed the faintest sign of freedom of the will was caned. It was almost impossible to avoid some form of punishment from the various teachers, nearly all women beyond the first flush of maidenhood. There was a Miss Barthwick, of yellow visage, and hair parted straight down the middle. She frequently called me out of the class and told me to hold out my hand. Then she would select a cane from a number of them, and " try it " by bending it on the desk in front of her. I was astounded that sometimes when she passed me in the street outside school hours she would give me a smile of kindly recognition. I could not believe that school teachers were capable of living private lives, of enjoying themselves, relaxing and absenting themselves from vigilance awhile.

Once only in my life have I wished to kill anybody. I edited a private paper, *The Boy's World*, written in an exercise-book, in patient and beautiful copper-plate handwriting ; I spent hours and hours over this labour of love on winter nights, a hundred pages, which I would circulate amongst my companions free of charge. I was author of all the serial stories, under various assumed names, emulative of Henry St. John. I invented a rival to Sherlock Holmes. His name was Dexter Deane ; no detective worth his salt owned to an ordinary Christian name such as George or Henry. I conducted an " Editor's Den " and occasionally followed the fashion of the boys' journals of the period by running a competition ; " missing words " or some such, awarding a first prize of £5 a week for life.

One day while I was surreptitiously handing round my periodical (fresh from the press) under cover of the desks, the teacher saw it, demanded to have it, and in front of the class she tore it into pieces—a rather lengthy task—and threw them into a waste-paper basket. If the wish to murder is a capital offence, I was then as guilty as any man that ever walked to the scaffold after eating a hearty breakfast. Perhaps a merciful judge would have acquitted me under the First Offender's Act. The teacher was one of the younger females of the staff. I remember her clearly to this day; she wore little oval spectacles, and when I caught a glimpse of the world through the edges of the lenses, as she stood near me, everything was very brilliant and small.

Our games were of our own arranging. We played cricket on the fields adjacent to the semi-slums in which I lived. They were not really fields; we called them "brickcrofts"; already the jerry-builder was at work upon "greater Manchester." There is a narrow street in Rusholme, my birth district, where a row of drab dwelling-places now stands, unless the Germans bombed them out of existence; and any summer evening some hot and hopeless housewife cooks the evening meal on the very spot where once we played over and over again Lancashire and Yorkshire matches witnessed at Old Trafford, or even a Test Match. We aped the heroes of the period. We began our games after "tea" and went on until total darkness. One evening I would announce that I was Lockwood and about to bowl fast; the next evening I might change myself to Rhodes and bowl so slowly that the ball scarcely reached the block-hole. It all depended upon what the day's county cricket scores chanced to reveal and extol.

I must have taken very early to the game. I can

clearly recall looking at the stop-press scores in the *Manchester Evening News*, and reading "Tyldesley, b. Anthony, 222," tidings of great joy from Trent Bridge, where Lancashire were that day playing "Notts." The date was round about 1900. It was certainly in this same summer that I entered the county cricket ground of Old Trafford for the first time, the first time of many.

More than forty years ago! Old Trafford was almost in the country then, Stretford was a village and there was no British Westinghouse. At the top of Warwick Road stood the Botanical Gardens; for some reason or other, gardens devoted to botany were supposed to serve as a means towards culture amongst the masses. I saw William Gunn in these gardens one evening; but I don't think he was studying botany. More than forty years ago, when a small boy nine years and three months old first saw the dread sign outside Old Trafford: "The public takes its own risk of the weather. No money returned." A year or two later, on a Saturday in July, 1902, I hesitated outside these forbidding gates; heavy rain-clouds darkened the sky. Then I heard a roar of agony from the crowd within and I risked my sixpence. This was the afternoon on which Australia won the rubber by three runs; I saw the collapse after Maclaren had fallen to a catch in the deep in an attempt to get the runs before the rain came. I think it is the truth that as Ranjitsinhji sat on the amateur's balcony waiting for his turn to bat on this afternoon of agony, he carved his initials on the window-ledge without knowing what he was doing. When in his turn he had to face Trumble and Saunders, he was marvellously and incredibly reduced to impotence, and failed miserably. This story is old and historical. The father of Maurice Tate came in when eight runs were needed, and by reflex action achieved four of them, then died the death. A year or so ago I saw and spoke to one of the few surviving members of this nobly tragic Test match, none other than Clem Hill, who caught out Lilley running yards and yards after what seemed a certain four from a low skimming drive. Hill claimed that he turned two somersaults after gripping the ball. Also he declared that Maclaren's language was spontaneous and empurpled.

They say it always rains at Old Trafford. But weather or industrial gloom or what not, the frieze of Old Trafford's cricket, the great sequence, comes back to mind as though lighted by eternal sunshine. Hornby and Barlow, the roaring ruddy Cheshire squire and his dour henchman. Briggs and his sad Grimaldi grimace; the stately Albert Ward, a whole Sunday School of batsmanship in himself. Maclaren, Spooner and J. T. Tyldesley, the three most brilliant batsmen that ever opened any county's innings one after the other. Walter Brearley, who bowled fast from morning till night until his eyes were coming out of his head and his face was as red as a boiled lobster. The rich Lancashire stuff of Harry Dean, Lol Cook, who always bowled into the wind, and knew that his demand for leg-before would fall on stone-deaf ears. Richard Tyldesley, emerging from three sweaters on a cold day; Duckworth crowing like a cock. I think I was the first man he ever stumped at Old Trafford; it was a so-called friendly match, and when I missed the ball and Duckworth shrieked his appeal and swept up all the bails and the stumps, I felt as though I had been sandbagged. And there was Parkin, lovable stormy petrel, spin and high spirits; when he was in form and getting wickets every over he used to sing comic songs.

Victor Trumper scored a century before lunch at Old Trafford in the same famous three runs Test Match of 1902. At Old Trafford, Ranjitsinhji not only ended his Test Match career but in 1896 performed there one of his most oriental conjurations against the Australian fast bowler, Ernest Jones; he glanced greased lightning from his left ear down to fine-leg for a four of a velocity rendered almost visible and luminous.

Another great Australian fast bowler—the most beautiful of them all—found his happiest hunting-ground at Old Trafford, his name McDonald, and his graceful ghost will be seen in the sunshine that falls on the next Lancashire and Yorkshire match played there. There were Makepeace and Watson, too, determined to stay in all day against Rhodes and Emmott Robinson; no boundaries before lunch, lads, on principle tha knows. Lancashire and Yorkshire, the greatest match of all, certainly the funniest. Think of it—Rhodes bowling protectively, with determination not to drop a ball anywhere within the hitting zone, bowling with all his cunning on a "safety-first" spot to a Makepeace who would have died rather than have hit the easiest half-volley—at any rate before lunch.

Many years ago, during the calmer moments of a

Lancashire v. Yorkshire match, I wrote a passage as follows: "At three o'clock there was no place on earth where I would rather have been than at Old Trafford. Sunshine fell on the field, and the venerable pavilion stood in the summer light; white clouds sailed in the sky and the Lancashire colours, with the Red Rose, fluttered in the gentle breeze. And the crowd indulged the old humours, never growing weary of them. Grand cheers greeted a piece of dashing fielding; roars fit to split the heavens went out when Lancashire passed the Yorkshire first innings total. A golden day, a noble crowd, and the greenest grass in England! Many a Lancashire man, exiled from this blessed country, now imprisoned across the seas, was thinking yesterday of Old Trafford and saying to his heart, 'Oh to be there—whoever's batting!'"

Those lines were written in August, 1926; and it is myself, as I write these lines, that am now the exiled one, far away in Australia, saying to his heart, "Oh to be there"; and saying also, "Greetings, Old Trafford, even if it's Lancashire that is still batting!"

It is a mystery to me that I was able in time to learn to play cricket more than competently. I was not physically strong, and my eyesight from the beginning was so myopic that a ball vanished into a mist in front of me after travelling a matter of thirty yards. No poor boy of the period would willingly wear spectacles; spectacles were considered a handicap to one's prospects at getting a job at a real "trade"; and no boy of the working classes was encouraged by his parents to become a clerk. There was no interest in cricket amongst my family. By temperament as well as by physique I was almost the last in the world ever to stand forth as an exponent of one of England's manly field sports. I cannot attempt to explain why by the time I was twenty years old I was proficient enough at cricket to make my living during summers as a professional. The point to be emphasised here is that it was through cricket that I escaped from the seemingly blind-alley of my lot in an existence as clerk, handy-man or any pitiful job; for I had no visible means of support, no technical training whatever, and no capacity to "rough it." Cricket opened my door of escape; cricket brought to me enough economic independence whereby to educate myself. That I was gifted to play the game, and to overcome weaknesses of temperament and physique, cannot plausibly be accounted for by any known theories of the influences of heredity or environment. A great county cricket ground was within reach of my home, true; but to watch a first match and to go from it and straightway knock a middle stump aslant almost without seeing it—this is another and different story.

I could not even join a club when I discovered my skill. The only available grounds in and round Manchester forty years ago were the privileges and possessions of the middle-classes. Half a mile from my backyard, where I bowled for hours at a bucket shielded by a broad piece of board, even as Albert Trott learned *his* arts of spin, was the beautiful cricket field of the Rusholme club. After I had gathered a little confidence in myself I would go there on summer evenings to field at net practice; the gentry were not above availing themselves of boys who were content to run about on a summer evening chasing balls and throwing them back to the bowler for not even a "thank you." Nobody dreamed of asking you to come forward for a trial. I hated them very much; and years afterwards when at last I played against Rusholme on this same delectable and green sward, I bowled them all out with a relish that counts amongst my most satisfying memories.

Imagine this youth, now beyond shy boyhood, thin and bespectacled but in possession of power over people at last. On a worn piece of turf I could spin an off-break without effort, so that it would whip upwards viciously straight at the most important and tender part of a man's anatomy. And not every player in those days used a "box." I am not ashamed to confess that I seldom hesitated, as soon as a batsman came to the crease, to let him have a quick one bang in the penis; after which a quick, simple straight one would invariably remove him from the scene.

I was not very good as a batsman because in the pre-spectacles stage of my career I could only play a back-stroke. I was obliged to wait for the bowling to pitch before I could see it, though I would crouch low, like Jessop, when the bowler began his attack, so that I might catch a glimpse of what was coming against the skyline. When I arrived at professional status, playing for clubs here and there and at Shrewsbury School, where I was assistant first to Attewell, then to Wainwright, I was content to bat number eleven, in which position I usually hit at least one boundary before succumbing. I do not remember ever scoring twenty runs without making three or four hits to the boundary.

My very first cricket match is as vivid in my mind more than forty years after as on the May afternoon of its occurrence. I was chosen as one of an eleven representing a theological training college in a Manchester district called Whalley Range. Why a theological training college took an interest in me I cannot tell. This team belonged to a league which fought out its battles on Saturday afternoons on pitches crude and unrolled, hard brown carth most amenable to spin. I firmly believe that on such a wicket in those halcyon years I could easily have bowled out an England eleven within a couple of hours.

The first ball I delivered for the theological training college was smitten for six, all run, by an uncouth denizen of Hulme, a slum adjacent to my native Rusholme. I was a passionate young man where my bowling was concerned, though I kept my feelings to myself. I never, as long as I took active part in cricket, summoned enough courage to appeal for leg-before wicket in an audible voice; but the sight of this huge hit off my first ball, a hit by a barbarian, and against the spin, too, the bat most horribly and blasphemously crooked, made me see red as seldom before and seldom afterwards. I "went through" the side forthwith; I took nine wickets for eight runs additional to the egregious six aforementioned.

But the theological training college lost the match.

They lost, as a fact, nearly every match in which I played for them, in spite or rather because of my unplayable spin. As I have written, the pitches were " nasty, brutish and short "—in a state of nature. No wicket-keeper extant could have prevented byes from bowling that transgressed all known laws of ballistics. As a consequence, though I would capture on an average seven or eight wickets every match for next to nothing, the " extras " would pile up so high a total that our batsmen were set a task beyond all reasonable hope of achievement. On these incalculable grounds 50 all out was a winning total. An inspection of the score-sheets of the theological training college would eloquently tell the same story every week; something like this:

Ancoats Settlement

Boggs, b. Cardus	4
Moggs, b. Cardus	0
Dodds, b. Cardus	2
Podds, b. Cardus	0
Stoakes, b. Cardus	1
Noakes, retired hurt	0
Stiles, b. Cardus	1
Thompson, b. Cardus ..	0
Wiffle, l.b.w., b. Tupman ..	1
Waffle, not out	0
Woffle, retired hurt	0
Extras	42
TOTAL .	51

Theological College

27 all out

At the end of the season, my first and last in this league, I took some 60 wickets for 80 runs ; and I was, I fancy, on the winning side once.

Such single-handed mastery I have not experienced since. My next season opened my eyes to my limitations. I played on rolled pitches, and to my astonishment discovered that the persuasiveness of my right forefinger was not all-powerful. To feel the leather spinning from the hand, to see the ideal flight and length—then the ball would go straight through, with time left for the batsman to make a drive past cover—past cover, mind you, off a potential breakback! . . . It is little wonder that this was the year of my absorption in philosophy.

Ah, but now came the most exquisite of the game's delights—the arduous cultivation of strategem, the patient preparation of a bowler's snare against a good batsman on a flawless pitch, the preliminary investigation of his tricks and the sizing-up of his temperament ; then the choosing of the likely bait and the subsequent angling, based on a "feeding" of his pet stroke ; it might all be spread over many overs and all the time you are terrified lest your captain should lose patience and take you off. At last the moment is here ; you drop the ball on the spot of your heart's desire ; sight, judgment and supple right arm and fingers are your sure ally ; the ideal length and spin are vouchsafed unto you—and the batsman "bites" and up she goes, a mishit to cover. If the catch is held, God's in his heaven ; fieldsmen stand round you in a circle, while you explain the trick ; the umpire (an old soldier) confidentially tells you he could see it all coming. The westering sun falls on your face, and while you are now resting awhile, you are aware that a breeze is running deliciously over your body. Many such times might a cricketer chant Nunc Dimittis; he may subsequently go through many varied days and experiences and nevermore will satisfaction, so deep and full, suffuse the whole of his being, and give him better reason to say "This is a good life!"

On the other hand, after the cunning unhurried laying of the decoy, cover-point might easily miss the catch, in which case all is ashes and unspeakable injustice and mortification. The poor fool of a fieldsman approaches you with a "Frightfully sorry, old chap—but she was spinning like——" and you are supposed to laugh it off with a "Well tried," or some such lie.

As I say, I did not bat seriously. But to be the official number eleven in the order of going in is not always irresponsibility and easy nerves and conscience. There are times when this batsman has to support an unreasonable burden, times when the weakest link in the chain is expected to withstand the severest strain. He may have to go to the wicket with a crucial question at stake of saving a "follow on"; worse still, he may have to face that most searching of mortal ordeals—eight to win and the last man in. Such a situation was my portion once on a calm day in Worcestershire, æons ago, during the golden age of country cricket reported every week in *The Field*; columns of scores and lovely names, "Somerset Stragglers," "Sussex Martlets," "Devonshire Dumplings," "Derbyshire Friars," or "Shropshire Gentlemen, with Thompson"—Thompson being the paid professional. On this calm day in June, I had bowled tolerably, and our eleven had been given not too many runs to score for victory. The wicket was good and we began well, so that when the tinkle of teacups sounded on the drowsy afternoon air, a tranquil end to the encounter was only a matter of time. After refreshment we all settled in our deck-chairs once more: I mean those of us occupying a place low down in the batting order. Pipes were lighted, and some dalliance with lady spectators was feasible, when suddenly a collapse began in the field before us, only a moment ago a field of formal procedure and rural decoration. A man of immense physical substance—I think he was Burrows the Worcestershire fast bowler—had returned to the attack with a new ferocity; stumps flew about like splinters. I was obliged to haul myself from a deck-chair, go into the dark dressing-room, and put on pads with my fingers fumbling, making a mess of straps and holes and buckles. All the time I secretly prayed that the batsmen now facing the music would endure and conquer. But no; I heard another sickening noise of a dismantled wicket in the failing light.

I walked down the wooden steps when we wanted exactly eight runs. Everything depended on me; the other batsman was our "crack"; he was seventy not out and well in charge of the bowling, even the bowling of the resurrected Burrows. A ripple of handclaps supposedly to encourage me came to my ear, but it was as noise from a far removed and very external universe; the world was now nothing but mine own fears and prayers. The long, lonely walk to the scene of crisis was ageing, and oh! the unfriendliness of everybody when I got there—most cricketers know of this sensation of bereft isolation. I began to take guard by force of habit, only to be told that the next ball would begin a new over from this end. Confusion and humiliation, and a public revelation of one's so far hidden poltroonery.

I must be ready to run, to collaborate with my masterful partner, to see that he obtained the bowling, and if possible always a single from the sixth ball. I might run him out. But these dread apprehensions were as naught to the actual happening; the master could not score a run at all in this first over, bowled to him as I backed up with my every nerve a pin-point of suspense. I was delivered unto Burrows, at the other end. I saw the ghostly fieldsmen changing position. I heard the remote umpire say "Two leg, sir." I felt somebody patting my block-hole; I felt a hand tightening the grip on my trousers above the left hip. A ventriloquial voice said, "A little closer, Harry." Then I saw Burrows looming and growing as he charged at me, larger and larger, a figure on the cinema that comes at you, widening and widening circles until the screen is overwhelmed and your vision is ready to burst into explosions of blinding nearness.

What to do? Play back or forward or not move an inch from the block-hole, or take courage and go for glory and swing the bat and to hell with it? Thought quicker than light shot through the brain. What in God's name to do?—but here is the ball, hot from muscle and temper, a ball of fire, a ball of—— Merciful heaven, it is nothing of the kind; it is a straight half-volley to the off. But dare I? If I mishit I shall be outcast, mocked at, the vainest of earthworms; but if I hit truly—— I did indeed hit truly. From the middle of the good blade, running up my arms, came sensations of joy beyond compare, music and tympani of nerves, vibrant to the brain and the heart; a four smack from the middle of the bat. A ball was thrown back from the distance, then I had a terrible momentary feeling of having looked over the rim of error into the void. Applause and shouts hailed me hero; and I experienced the illusion of a growth in actual stature.

Next, anti-climax; for there were more balls to face alone from Burrows, now outraged and silent. Four to win, remember. Again he strides and again the mighty arm swings. Gloria in Excelsis, if it isn't a long-hop this time, to leg! I couldn't believe my eyes. And nobody placed deep on that side of the field. I must not falter; Burrows already is cursing his folly, vowing revenge next ball, if I miss this chance worth a soul's ransom. I do not understand why I did not excitedly cleave the air "too soon," but I didn't. I waited until the ball was "leaving me"; then I struck it almost from behind. No more certain boundary hit has been executed; the ball went there quicker than from the bat. I had "won the match" in two blows myself. And I did not wake up; it was not a dream. Thirty-five years ago, and true and real this present minute. I can see it all, the formal chase of a fieldsman after my decisive stroke; he ran only a few yards. The cheering and the intense relief to mind and nerve. Then at once the feeling that it is over, and will never come back, the actual ecstatic doing of it, never . . .

Other games, they tell me, have their like felicities and their crowns of thorns. No cricketer believes it; no cricketer, if he is honest, will admit that of all the pleasures he may dwell upon in the evening of his days, any one will return with the poignancy of those vanished hours on the summer field; for we can, to the very end, partake of other delights, of reading and music and wine and conversation and candlelight and even of love. But sure as sure, the day will come too soon when (happily he never knows it) the cricketer hits a ball for the last time, bowls a ball for the last time, fields a ball for the last time, and for the last time walks home with his companions to the pavilion in the evening glow, his sweater flung across his shoulders.

It was strange but not marvellous that a poor boy with a frail physique and a shy, nervous disposition and of extreme short sight should in time have come to play cricket; for after all this is our national game. Sooner or later everybody belonging to England will be tempted to succumb to its allurements. But I can attribute the music discovered in me late in my teens only to some obscure hereditary influence. There was no piano in my home, or any other instrument; the radio was not yet a universal disseminator of music, and the phonograph remained more or less experimental and sepulchral. The piano was, indeed, in these days the privilege of the middle and upper-classes; I was at least eighteen years old before I entered a house containing a piano ; and the top of it was covered with family portraits. The only music taught in the Board school was tonic-solfa—doh, ray, me—which I found more than useful when I began really to learn to read a score ; I once transposed or translated nearly a whole piano arrangement of " Tristan and Isolde " into tonic-solfa (the last sharp to the right a " te " ; the last flat to the right a " fah "). Four-part songs were sung in school a half an hour or so a week, conducted by one of the corsetted yellow faces ; sometimes we had to read tonic-solfa at sight, not only from the blackboard but from various signs made by the teacher's hand. " Doh " was a fist clasped strenuously ; " ray " was the right hand slightly aslant, as though in disapproval ; and so on. The songs we sang included " As pants the hart for cooling streams " and Balfe's " Excelsior."

When the music was written in tonic-solfa on the blackboard, coloured chalks denoted the different voices, alto and treble. And when the singing-class was at an end the blackboard would be turned over and the reverse side used for other and more practical studies, such as long division. Once I was hauled out of class for some misdemeanour, and hidden out of the sight of my kind, girls as well as boys, segregated in two groups ; and I was put behind this blackboard. The teacher left the class-room for a while, and I took some coloured chalks from her desk and altered at random the tonic-solfa notation, changing " fahs " to " rays," or " tes " to " lahs." The following week, when the class sang " As pants the hart " at sight, empirical efforts in atonalism were heard for the first time in England. I was easily identified as the cause of the dissonances, and I was—probably fairly and with justice for once in a way—prodigiously flogged.

My mother and her sisters frequented the variety theatres, and while they went about their housework they sang tunes out of *The Geisha*, *San Toy* and Leslie Stuart. The ramifications of the melody of " Tell me, Pretty Maiden " left them rather at a loss. No popular music has equalled the beautiful and unexpected phrasing and transitions of this part-song in *Florodora*. The tunes of musical comedy and variety theatre of the late 'nineties and nineteen-hundreds had charm and art enough to awaken a child's sensibilities to music proper. James Agate has told us how by slowing down the rhythm and using German words, " Bleibt die Mutter bei dir immer," he has deceived serious musicians into thinking that " Is your Mammy always with you ? " was a cradle song by Brahms discovered lining a drawer in his bedroom of the Tiergarten Hotel in Berlin. To take delight, at a theatre alive and animated and full of colour, in the music of *La Cloche de Corneville*, *La Poupée*, *Veronique*, *The Little Michus* and later the operettas of Fall, Oscar Straus and Lehar, was an attractive way of approach to the authentic masters, more likely to lead somewhere than the self-conscious appreciation classes of current middle-class fashion on the one hand ; and on the other the croonings of Bing Crosby which have taken the place of the popular music of Leslie Stuart, and also that of anonymous bards who composed " My Tiger Lily "—sung by Amy Height at one of Robert

Courtneidge's Prince's Theatre pantomimes in the 1900's: Amy Height was a negress, and she did not croon—and "A Military Man" and the "Hiawatha" song, which was used as a march for *The Forty Thieves* in another Christmas pantomime at the Prince's Theatre. To this present moment I can recapture the accumulation of excitement during the cave scene in *Aladdin*, when our hero couldn't remember the magic word to open the door, and the phrases of the march "Hiawatha," thrummed pianissimo, increasing to a fortissimo crescendo, played by a real orchestra and not a Wurlitzer organ, heralded the gradual approach of the dreaded enemy. Every boy who went to the theatre then tried to get near enough to the orchestra to see the players come from under the stage, stooping low so as not to bang their heads. Unconcernedly they would take their seats and arrange the faded pieces of their music, written as though spiders and flies had walked over the pages after having escaped from ink-pots, pages held together with gummed paper. They would tune up as though not yet thoroughly masters of the mechanics of trombone and trumpet; the conductor took his seat after bowing to the audience who recognised him as an artist in his own right. Now and again, while the dialogue or action of the piece needed no musical supports, a player here and there would crane his head upwards, even to standing on tiptoe, to catch a glimpse of what was transpiring on the stage; but as a rule the orchestra showed to the play and the performance an indifference which always struck me as uncanny and abnormal. It is curious, or maybe it isn't, that the

Savoy operas scarcely influenced the course of my musical taste, though I heard much of them and liked them up to a point. But Sullivan did not warm my senses or moisten my eyes ; I was never intoxicated by the sound of his music, as I was one night during the interval of a play by Charles McEvoy, called *David Ballard*, presented at the Midland Theatre by Miss Horniman (this was the beginning of her repertory seasons in Manchester). A small orchestra was directed by a Viennese musician named Drescher, and as I sat alone in the back seats, admission a shilling, waiting impatiently for the curtain to rise on Act 2, I became conscious for the first time in my life of the romantic power of muted strings, as the melody of the Vilia song from *The Merry Widow* curled its way into my heart to stay there for a lifetime ; I can take it out like old lavender ; it is not now a musical possession but an aromatic association. I believe that this was a good way to educate latent taste, better than abstract analysis of sonata-form in advance of an imaginative and sensuous experience of what a composer expresses through sonata-form.

But I read a lot about music before actually I knew music itself. I discovered Ernest Newman ; he was music-critic of the *Manchester Guardian* in 1905, then he went to the *Birmingham Post*. I read him in the library newsroom. At this time he wrote with enthusiasm and prejudice ; he made my mouth water by his description of Gerhardt before I had ever even heard of her ; he described Aino Akté as " Salome " in the language that tingled the blood, and he went on to inflame my mind by saying that though music had lost much since Mozart, it had gained much in knowledge of good and evil. I, with thousands of young men, owe more to the *Manchester Guardian* for the fact that at the right impressionable period, the arts were related for us to tangible and multi-coloured life. Montague, Agate, Monkhouse and Newman—there were never more suggestive and stimulating day-by-day openers of doors and magic casements than these. If they all, except Monkhouse, over-wrote occasionally, that was much to the good; it's a poor fire that won't blaze under provocation. The main point is that it was in a daily newspaper we could warm our minds; every morning at breakfast, and on the tops of trams. Books are books and they need searching out. But imagine that you are looking into the day's news, glancing at this and that report upon various and evanescent terrestrial occurrences, and you turn a page and run into a whole column about a performance of *Richard II*, with F. R. Benson the King. And this is what you read:

> "What exactly is it in a man that makes an artist of him? Well, first a proneness in his mind to revel and bask in its own sense of fact; not in the use of fact—that is for the men of affairs, the Bolingbrokes; nor in the explanation of fact—that is for the men of science; but simply in his own quick and glowing apprehension of what is about him, of all that he has done on the earth or goes on in the sky, of dying and being born, of the sun, clouds, storms, of great deeds and failures, the changes of the seasons, and the strange events of men's lives. To mix with the day's diet of sights and sounds the man of this type seems to bring a wine of his own that lights a fire in his blood as he

sits at the meal. . . . To shun the dry light, to drench all he sees with himself, his own temperament, the humours of his own moods—this is not his dread but his wish, as well as his bent. 'The eye sees what the eye brings the means of seeing.' 'A fool sees not the same tree that a wise man sees.' 'You shall see the world in a grain of sand and heaven in a wild flower.' This heightened and delighted personal sense of fact, a knack of seeing visions at the instance of seen things, is the basis of art. Only the basis, though. For that art may come a man must add to it a veritable passion for arresting and defining in words, or lines and colours, or notes of music, not each or anything that he sees, nor anybody else's sense of that thing, nor yet the greatest common measure of many trained or untrained minds' senses of it, but his own unique sense of it, the precise quality and degree of emotion that the spectacle of it breeds in him and nobody else, the net result of its contact with whatever in his own temperament he has not in common with other men. That is the truth of art, to be true less to facts without you that to yourself as stirred by facts."

The Pater cadence, of course:

"Every moment some form grows more perfect in hand or face; some tone on the hills and the sea is choicer than the rest; some mood or passion of insight or intellectual excitement is irresistibly real and attractive to us—for that moment only. Not the fruit of experience, but experience itself, is the end. A counted number of pulses only is given to us of a variegated, dramatic life. How may we see in them all that is to be seen in them by the finest senses?"

But Pater in precious volumes and Montague any

Tuesday morning! What is more, all these rubies and pulsations of language and high life were not the perquisite of a set, a fashion, a "movement"; most intelligent folk of Manchester and Lancashire read the "M.G."; and I have seen many an album of cuttings from the paper, family possessions in the grim stone houses of self-made mill-owners of Blackburn, Leigh and Colne, dour Liberals who began their education at a Mechanics' Institute (as my grandfather began his); transition to the delighted pagan æsthetic of Montague probably was an effort and a shock; but they took it. And I, and several youths of my own social station, galleryites and attenders of free lectures at the Art Gallery and the Islington Hall, would no more have missed reading Montague, Agate, Monkhouse, Newman and Langford than we would have missed Maclaren at Old Trafford, or Forbes Robertson or Richter or Eugene Stratton.

Years after, when by incalculable spinnings of fate I had become music-critic of the *Manchester Guardian*, I knew one of these old Liberals, "jannock" Lancashire men who formed the basis of the paper's circulation, and scrutinised each column with jealous eyes to be sure the standards were being kept up; there were hundreds and hundreds like him, and they would come to Manchester every morning by the 7.50, seated behind the broad pages of "t' *Guardian*," and from time to time certain clicks of satisfaction would be heard, perhaps even a downright verbal utterance: "Montague's hittin' 'ard" or "Scott's a bit stiff to-da-ay."

This Liberal I came to know was a gaunt hatchet-faced man who, after the 1914-1918 war, occupied each week a side corner seat not far from mine at the Hallé Concerts in a cheaper part of the hall. It was a time of ruin in the Lancashire mills, and every Thursday evening I would see this man come to his place, looking worn and worried; then when the music began, his eyes would close, and at the end of a composition they sometimes opened as though from shock; and he never applauded. One evening, he approached me in the interval and, with dignity but obvious nervousness, introduced himself and wished to shake hands with the *Guardian's* critic; he had known Newman and Langford; in fact, he "went back to George Fremantle." He was in the mid-sixties and he carried that morning's *Guardian* in his hand. He had of course read it at breakfast and on the train coming to town, also during his snatched lunch, but he would go through it more carefully on the way home and after he'd got there. Later he asked me to give an address to the "Literary Society" of the town in which he lived; he was the founder and the chairman. I went there on a bitter night in winter. The mills were black and vacant; some of them had no window-panes. My audience was made up of men and women of all ages, some in cloth caps and shawls, some in white winged collars (the Elders), nearly all of them showing signs that they were feeling the pinch. I talked about the songs of Hugo Wolf, using gramophone records for illustrations. I have never since spoken to an audience so quick of apprehension, and so absorbed and moved at times—and at others so palpably not to be taken in by immoderate speech.

At the end of the lecture, my chairman asked me to his home for supper; a house of stone, built ages ago. Soon he would have to give it up. His wife died shortly after his son had been killed in the Somme massacres, a year after he had left Rossall School. "He would have gone to one of the Universities," said my host, who himself had been a "half-timer" as a boy of ten. He had educated himself; I saw his books: Darwin, Huxley, Tyndall, Mill (both of them), Ricardo, Buckle, Spencer; *Sesame and Lilies* and *Unto This Last*, Leslie Stephen and Bagehot, Dickens, Thackeray, Scott, Eliot and the rest, with an advance up to *One of Our Conquerors* of Meredith, and a complete Shaw. Then in another shelf, a number of musical scores, symphonies, oratorios and piano arrangements of *Tristan* and the "*Ring*"—but no actual piano music, except the Beethoven sonatas.

He had worked his way up from a half-timer to a mill-manager. He had given all his days and many of his nights to it; he would "go down to t' mill" even on Sundays "for just a look and see if all was right." Then the war came and the crash of all that he, staunch believer in the ultimate brotherhood and rationalism of man, had cherished in his austere heart and mind. Now he was in fallen circumstances; the house had to go; he would put it all into auctioneers' hands, live in lodgings and take up an agency. But he'd keep his old yellow-keyed upright piano, a Collard and Collard; and if he couldn't buy a subscriber's ticket to next year's "Hallé," he'd go "in shilling places," where he'd begun, in times when "Norman-Neruda played

Mendelssohn violin concerto like you never hear it played now, so fine and delicate and so like sunshine on t' hillside over yon, when it shines at all." There was no self-pity, no bitterness. "Ah've had a good life," he said; "and Ah've got something there"—tapping his head—"that they can never take from me in a hurry."

As we sat in his sitting-room, I saw the worn spots on the carpet near his writing-desk. I saw a life's rubbings against chair-backs, a life's openings of doors and a life's pickings-up of cinders from the hearth, a life's usage on the solid table and sideboard. After supper he took me to my train, a half a mile's walk across the moor, and thanked me for coming to talk to his Society. "You could see," he said, "that they were liking it. No coughing. Aye; they were liking it." It was the best compliment he could make to me; they had "liked" Hugo Wolf in a depressed area, on a cold night in an unwarmed room of the local Sunday School.

The circulation of the *Manchester Guardian* in time spread to Hampstead and other haunts of culture, where a concerto for Tabor, Harpsichord and Blowpipe by Septimus Poppit is of more import than the whole of the works of Wagner put together. But the "M.G." in Scott's day, the high noon and glory, was fundamentally built on the taste, the prejudice, the grudging hard-to-win but honest and intense support of such men of Lancashire county as him I have here tried to describe.

He, of course, knew of Islington Hall, Ancoats; he

was, he vowed, one of the original audience, before the gentry of Altrincham and Bowdon ever heard of it. Islington Hall was situated in Ancoats, Manchester, one of the worst slums produced during a prosperous epoch in our island story. Islington Hall on Sundays was supposed to supply culture to the working-man. The guiding spirit was Charles Rowley, a complete example of nineteenth-century ameliorist, one of the Morris school and so pre-Raphælitish in his appearance and opinions that as he grew older and older he more pronouncedly and comically resembled somebody out of a drawing by Ford Madox Brown. Rowley did not himself paint; but he did the next best thing and sold pictures and picture-frames in a shop. He went rambles all over the lakes—one of the first of the "fresh-air fiends" of the century; he probably climbed the Matterhorn, reading Whymper. On Sunday afternoons he lorded it over us in a large hall up a flight of stone steps. The district of Ancoats and its temple of culture were approached through underworld railway arches that were dark and long enough to be called tunnels, then we emerged into narrow streets lined with back-to-back houses. The peacefulness of Sunday afternoons amongst the original denizens of Ancoats was disturbed by the procession of carriages and cars conveying the bulk of Rowley's audience from the stately homes of Bowdon and Victoria Park, all of them Forsytes eager to listen to a concert and a famous speaker at the cost of a piece thrown into a "silver collection." The natives of Ancoats proper did not rally in large numbers round Rowley; they (or those not lying indoors prone on sofas in their shirt-sleeves) sat at front-door steps, and contemplated the passing show or listened to the spittings of pipes and valves in the engine-rooms of the temporarily moribund factories, or inhaled the perfume of the adjacent wharves.

Every week between October and March, I walked four miles to Ancoats on Sundays and four miles back. It was at the " Ancoats Brotherhood " that I first heard Egon Petri play Beethoven's Op. 111 ; on the same occasion Bernard Shaw spoke about the Ten Commandments, and he was not then regarded as respectable. As he stood on the platform, arms akimbo, in tweeds and with still the red flame of Socialism in his beard, he told us to burn down the Manchester Town Hall and the Cathedral, for some reasons I can't remember but they were strictly reformative ; and having digressed a while from the theme of his discourse, said, " But now, ladies and gentlemen ; let's return to our old friend God." I didn't know at the time that this was a cheap joke ; we revelled in the outrageousness of it, we had been repressed so long in our public discussions of the Almighty. Even the atheists of the period shilly-shallied, as Lady Bracknell might have observed : they called themselves agnostics. I remember nothing else of Shaw's talk that day except that I was electrified by the tempo, charmed by the accent and twinkle, astounded that anybody could say so much without a manuscript, an hour of it and not a fumble, not the omission of a semi-colon, of speech.

Then Petri, a young man teaching at the Royal Manchester College of Music, brought Beethoven into the hall like a living presence, just as the November day was darkening. I think it was my baptism into music as a spiritual fact. I did not understand the language, but I heard the voice. Next day, or some time after, Langford in the *Guardian* told me what I had heard.

> ". . . those various transitions and ranges of emotion for the height and parallel of which we could go nowhere in poetry but to the ' Paradiso ' of Dante. We have likened that apotheosis of the shake with which this sonata ends and in which the whole mechanical construction and subtlety of the work finds its solution, to those studies of light with which Turner in his last years baffled his beholders. The comparison is not far-fetched, nor yet the comparison with the moving glass, the smoothest of all poetic rhythms, in which Dante turns his divine verse. . . . The final variations approach so nearly to a mechanical perfection that the contemplation of its nearness almost brings a shudder to the mind. Yet where shall we find music more divinely separated from the mechanical than in the first variations, whose whole existence seems to be the blissful stirring of an inward life."

This was education, if you like! To hear great music unfolded one day, and next day to read these wise thoughts, so unforgettable, in simple but subtle statement . . ." comparison with the moving glass, the smoothest of all poetic rhythms in which Dante turns his divine verse." There was only one thing for it now —to learn Italian, and read Dante in the original; meanwhile one had to put up with Cary.

Charles Rowley would sit at the right-hand side of the speaker. Himself, he made the same speech every week. He would thank the distinguished visitor and the musicians, saying that Pierpont Morgan himself couldn't have commanded finer gifts, such oratory or a grander concert. He went on to tell us how he had made his friend Shaw swallow a lifetime's principle and travel all the way to Manchester to give a lecture on Sunday—" free gratis and for nothing, give it here, mind you, in the depths of Ancoats, not amongst the nobs. He wrote to me saying, ' I'll see you damned before I come to Ancoats, Sabbath or any other day,' and I replied, ' My dear Shaw, I'm not arguing with you, I'm telling you. So give me a date and save both your time and mine.' And here, ladies and gentlemen —here he is.' " Then Rowley would, for the thousandth time, put his famous resolution : " Mr. Shaw and Mr. Petri have given us the afternoon of our lives. Pierpont Morgan—I repeat it—couldn't do better. The resolution before the meeting is that Mr. Shaw and Mr. Petri are jolly good fellows, and that we are damned lucky to have them here with us to-day. Those in favour will say ' Aye.' " (The meeting would roar their approval.) " Now," Rowley would command, " the ' Noes.' " And after listening carefully to the ensuing silence, cocking his ear and putting his hand behind it so justice might be done to any nervous dissentient at the back of the hall, he would say, as though open to correction even at the last moment, " I *believe* the ' Ayes ' have it." Sometimes, at the last of a season's gatherings of the Ancoats Brotherhood, Rowley would lead us in parting song, conducting from the platform like a prophet. And we would sing the unison of :

"*Bring me my bow of burning gold,*
Bring me my arrows of desire;
Bring me my spear! O clouds unfold,
Bring me my chariot of fire.

I shall not cease from mental fight,
Nor shall my sword sleep in my hand,
Till we have built Jerusalem
In England's green and pleasant land."

A young man that once was myself sang these words with such emotion that when he descended the stone staircase into Ancoats, with the departing throng, he could scarcely see, as he began his homeward journey, left behind by the carriages, through the tunnels, into the thickening Manchester night; the denizens all indoors and the street lamps yellow and solitary.

Rowley lived to a fabulous age and saw the vanishing of the first view of the earthly paradise in which the swords were to have been turned into ploughshares. But I am certain that he died in the belief that the "Ayes," sooner or later, would "have it."

∗ V ∗

I COULD not afford to go to learn an instrument at the Royal Manchester College of Music but I never missed a concert given there, every fortnight, by students, free of charge, programme one penny. All the professors attended and sat on the front row, while youths and girls played and sang. The next day the critic of the *Manchester Guardian* mentioned none of the artists by name but referred to them this way: "a pupil of the Principal hinted of intelligence," or "a girl under Mr. Mayer was promising" . . . and so forth. The Principal, as we all know, was Dr. Brodsky, a Russian with a genial wind-scrubbed face, but of no certain temper. He shuffled about the Manchester streets, gone at the knees, and many a time I saw him emerging from the "Delicatessen" shop at the corner of Ducie Street, a few yards from the College building, carrying a parcel of things good to eat and drink. He lived well and had no inhibitions. It is said that girl students sometimes came out of his class-room gulping and blind with tears, while young men turned pale and went below to the lavatories and were sick. But he would beam like the rising sun when next he met those he had called horrible names. It did not occur to him or to little Max or to any of the teaching staff that students attended the College to learn to perform in public some day at concerts and earn large fees; that is a more recent idea of the end and purpose of the life musical. The true gardener does not tend his growths to produce a prize rose. "You come here to lof music," said Brodsky to his classes; "and if you lof music you will make the right notes and play the lofely tones; and if you are virtuose von day it will be very nice for you and the audience; but it is moch better when you lofe music, and if you are girls and ver' pretty it is better for you to haf babies and play for them, so they will grow up and lof music."

Sometimes Langford, looking like a cross between Socrates and Moussorgsky, loose in his old clothes as an elephant, would come to a students' concert and not send a deputy; and he would listen to Beethoven and forget the intonation and what not, and go to the *Guardian* office and write nearly a column of wise and devoted meditation, almost omitting to mention he'd been to a concert at all. He would bend his great head on his chest, and finger a sonata, as one was being played, on the arm of his chair. And he would produce from a bottomless pit of a shabby coat a broken magnifying-glass, the frame gone years since, and scan his programme through it.

I heard the "Dichterliebe" for the first time at the Royal Manchester College of Music, sung by a Francis Harford; his voice was without tone; it was undecided of pitch, but he was an artist. I think the piano parts were played by an extremely good-looking girl named

Dorothy Crewe. It was, I remember, Miss Fillunger who, also out of tune, revealed to me Hugo Wolf; and I rushed away to the library and borrowed Newman's book and learned it by heart; but did not think the less of Schubert, for all that.

On several Saturday afternoons every year, the Brodsky Quartet played, and I got there early and sat at the back of the hall for a shilling. Brodsky's colleagues, like himself, looked exactly right; they were as though an old engraving had come to life—" The Musicians "—Simon and Sam Speelmann and Carl Fuchs, walrus moustache and spectacles, and Simon's viola was velvet and matured sunshine; they all sat down and got themselves ready, tapping the music pages on the stands with their fiddle-sticks; or dancing the bows tentatively on the strings while Fuchs investigated the deeps of his 'cello. Brodsky was the best player I have known in a late Beethoven quartet; his violin seemed to receive the music, not play it. He did not make a god of technique; nowadays he might even be called uneven and thin of tone. But he was technically good when it was necessary so to be. It was as though a current of Beethoven's thought were running down his strings, free and not connived; pulsations of a mind never fastidious, each note in quick passages leaping by its own will and animation, defying a fixed pitch. It was as though Brodsky were going beyond the printed symbols and quavers and semi-quavers to the source of musical life itself; the form was not one of prosaic and chain-like details of perfection, but of an energy which " thrilled in each nerve and lived along the line." Nobody has played the Cavatina quartet as Brodsky and his colleagues played it in those days. Better still, because the music is even more divine, was their playing in the D flat Lento of Op. 135; here was the melody of perfect peace for Fuchs to nurse and cradle; then came the falling aerial showers of notes for Brodsky; and his tone surrendered all material substance, all semblance of ordered limited and arranged contours, "sounds of such fineness that they are like the moist particles of air on the loveliest summer mornings."

The afternoon's twilight suited the strains of the wisest tenderest music in existence; Brodsky pressed his fiddle more and more to himself, Fuchs looked into some strange and habited vacancy as he played the undertones; and Speelmann was moist of mouth and moustache. Everything was so secure and intimate as we all sat here, with ancient instruments hanging on the college walls; then at the end, Brodsky and his colleagues came before us bowing and smiling, moving aside for one another to pass when they left the platform. As I dwell on these Saturday afternoons I am again overwhelmed, against all sense and logic, by the fact that these things which once happened and were so seemingly permanent should ever have ended, and vanished from the face of the earth. The close communion of the music-room, the presence of friends met every day, the low distant murmur of Manchester's traffic, Brodsky and his fiddle, the sane keen winter wind that met our faces when we came out of the concert, the glow of the Delicatessen window at the corner, the chuckles and talk of the professors, now getting into a cab to go to Oxford Road station, to take a train for Bowdon and the home of Brodsky, where awaited the cosy log-fire and hearthrug, the sherry on the sideboard, and the safe twinkling harbour of hospitality . . . " the delicious juices of meats and fishes, and society, and the cheerful glass, and candlelight, and fireside conversation, and innocent vanities, and jests, and irony itself—do these things go out with life ? "

It was Harford, when he sang the " Dichterliebe " cycle of Schumann, who made me decide to try to become a great Lieder singer ; like Harford I had little tone in my voice, so his example was encouraging. This was a period which was in violent reaction against what was called (by those of us then " reacting ") mere voice ; I found a phrase of Berlioz and grew strong and superior on it : " Performers on the larynx." The intellectual school of vocalism trusted to brains ; we despised the Carusos and Tetrazzinis. " The higher the voice the lower the intellect "—so wrote Ernest Newman, about somebody ; and we applauded—at least I did. Still, even the intellectual school of singing insisted on *some* vestige of voice, so I was obliged to see what could be done about it. As I couldn't pay yet for singing lessons I consulted the library once more. At random, for I knew nothing of the subject of voice production, I hit upon a book by Emil Behnke, with illustrations showing the insides of the lungs and throat, all abstract, removed from any personal identity and very vivid. " Chubes ! " as Mr. Polly said.

One of Behnke's vocal exercises involved the repetition of " Koo, koo, koo, koo, koo—oo—oh—ah " on eight repeated notes of the same pitch throughout one's range, the idea being to "place" the voice forward. A lot was written in those days by experts in voice-production about "placing." There were breathing exercises too; I would stand in front of an open window, at break of dawn, and take in a Manchester fog, releasing the air very slowly until I nearly burst myself. Another breathing exercise was performed lying prone on one's back, looking at the ceiling. I paid a widowed woman in the back-street hovel of Hulme a shilling each time to allow me use of an unfurnished attic one night every week; and I climbed the rickety stairs, carrying a candle in a candlestick, for the attic had no means of illumination and the night was sure to be pitch black and cold as charity. I used a tuning-fork to keep my bearings. Up and down the scale I koo-koo-oh-ah'd for an hour, advancing my studies gradually to herculean attempts at crescendi on sustained chest-notes. Also I practised while walking along the Manchester streets when other pedestrians were not too close to me. The roar of the traffic easily concealed my *coup de glotte*. But now and again a sudden lull would occur in the city's roar; a tram would stop and create a vacuum in which I was exposed—or as the music-hall comedians used to say, "left"—on a strangled high E flat; I never could really cope with anything higher than D. I was a circumscribed baritone.

I made some unaccountable progress and actually began to get an engagement or two. This was the time of the "grand" concerts on Saturday nights in parochial halls; there was no cinema to entertain the lower middle-classes. Of course I was compelled to compromise my intellectual notions about the function of song: I could not attempt German Lieder at a "smoker" for the local Freemasons. In my repertory was included "numbers" by Herman Lohr, J. Airlie Dix, Noel Johnson: "Grey days are your grey eyes, and when the rainbow comes, that is your smile"—the "smile" vanishing into complete but still open-mouthed inaudibility, while the piano trembled to the conclusion. Occasionally I risked some idealism and sang the "Freebooter" songs of William Wallace, including "Son of Mine," in which the word "sheep" had to be sung on high E, so I changed it (for the purposes of firmer vocal grip) into "shape." After a bout of serious vocalism, I would, according to the customs, relax into coyness—"Och, the de-arr Oirish girl," or "Trottin' to the Fair." Once I even took part in that most absurd of duets, "Madam, will you walk?"; and I addressed a female of gathering years with "O I shall geeve you the keys of heaven." I studied all the details of the platform manner of Kennerley Rumford. I would stand in front of the piano and give the accompanist a polite encouraging and gently condescending smile, a sign for him to begin.

But in my own way, and in my own time, I made myself acquainted with a great range of Lieder and I enjoyed the experience and profited. To my delight I discovered one day a song by Cornelius which might have been composed specially for me; it suited my range, and my expressive scope. It was "Eine Monotone." So deeply did I sink myself in music hereabout that I even neglected my beloved cricket. To this day

I can remember most important details in the history of cricket except any concerning the four summers of 1908 to 1912; I have to consult "Wisden" when these seasons are under discussion. I actually did not go to the Test Matches at Old Trafford in 1909, and I was nineteen years old—and Victor Trumper was playing! No, I was lost in music; it has always been my practice to go into a subject until I am obsessed and possessed by it, immersed head to foot.

I went to my first Hallé Concert in the winter of 1908, and Santley sang "O ruddier than the cherry." I waited in a queue for the shilling area, a narrow confine at the back of the Free Trade Hall, where a heating apparatus known as the "Grid" erupted fumes of a volcanic nature. Santley, past his seventieth year, looked somehow Old Testamentish, though he had no beard, only a white moustache and a cloud of white hair. His tone and phrasing were still wonderful, and each word he sang could be heard without need to strain an ear. He also sang on this occasion "It is enough" from the *Elijah* with great sincerity; but he was didactic rather than poignant, a sort of vocal pre-Raphaelite, a singing Holman Hunt. His technique, of course, would nowadays render him not only incomparable but unique. Vocalists of this period in England made little attempt as a whole to create the illusion of impersonal absorbed art; they came before the audiences socially conscious. Ben Davies wore white gloves and a flower in his button-hole. This is an amenity of the concert-hall which has been preserved to the present day by Sir Malcolm Sargent. At performances of oratorio, the male singer gallantly escorted the soprano and the contralto to their chairs on the platform—Madame This or Madame That—and, while the overture was being played to the *Messiah*, all four of them would sit there perusing their vocal scores and looking appropriately devotional.

My career as a singer came to an end a year or so after I had delivered myself into the care of the teachers of voice production. I do not indict them altogether; the odds were against them, no doubt; but before consulting them I at least could produce, even if only ventriloquilly, the impression that a singer really was somewhere about or around. After a dozen or so lessons I was reduced to a state of what might be called congestion of the larynx. And, of course, as I tried different professors in turn, each assured me that I had come to him "just in time." I was instructed by one master to practise on the vowel A, only to be told by another that my urgent need was the sound OO; another advocated the *coup de glotte*; another threw up his hands in horror at the very mention of it. I was introduced to nasal resonance and made stiff of chin. I was rendered tongue-conscious. I had so far not been aware that the tongue possessed the power to waggle and flop about the mouth by its own volition. From the moment I was told that a singer, while enunciating "ah" must keep his tongue flat and still, with the tip relaxed next the lower teeth, my tongue clove to the roof of my mouth. I was made to hold a lighted candle and to sing scales at it; if it fluttered in the slightest, something needed doing to "concentrate" my tone. I suppose there was a grain of sense in all this quackery ; and I suppose it is still taught and swallowed. My own experience of the teachers of singing, the voice-builders and so on, is that they have little more wisdom to impart than that, granted a good voice from nature, a student will go ahead if he keeps the muscles of his chin and throat free and not clenched, trains his ear, controls his diaphragm, and has nothing whatever to do with theories of vocal colour, but allows his imagination to do the shading.

It is good to know and savour the good moment before it has passed and not to have to wait until memory in a sort of index of experience directs attention to the best things that have happened in a lifetime. Most of us are dependent on some such sifting ; none of us is able always to cry out, "Verweile doch, du bist so schön !" at the right time. I thank my fortune that when Hans Richter lived in Manchester, and could any day be seen in the city streets, probably on Thursday noons after a rehearsal with the Hallé orchestra ambling along Peter Street to the Continental Restaurant, I thank my stars that I knew that the sight of him was terrific, momentous, historical and legendary. He had known Wagner, had copied out the first score of *Meistersinger*, had taken part in that incomparable serenade on Christmas morning at Triebschen, when the Meister gathered all the musicians together on the staircase, and Cosima had been wakened, as no woman has since or ever again will be wakened.

Wagner was still close to us in the England of 1910 and thereabouts. If his sun was beginning to set it was only to redden deeper and deeper the whole sky of our music. *The Ring* had not yet been heard in England outside London; but it was enough for a Manchester boy to go to the Hallé concerts and hear a platform version of Act III of *Meistersinger*, and nobody has equalled the Richter breadth and German ease of tempo in *Meistersinger*. I forget who it was who sang the "Wahn! Wahn!" monologue the first time I ever heard it, perhaps David Bispham; and the crescendo at the end remains unparalleled: "nun aber kam Johannistag" and "nie ohn' ein'gen Wahn gelingen."

Music was not yet a common possession; a Hallé concert was a privilege hard to share. To listen to Wagner and Beethoven, conducted by Richter, was to know that much was being added to one's stature, and that somehow one had been called and chosen out of many. To gaze on Richter was to experience wonder; I once followed in his footsteps as he shambled along the pavement and I tried to fit my boots exactly in the places trodden by him. He had spoken to Wagner; and no composer since has meant so much to the imagination as Wagner meant to those of us who in 1910 had just come of age and were listening to the Hallé orchestra, under Richter, beginning the *Meistersinger* overture, "broad as ten thousand beeves at pasture," straight from the incredible mint.

There was a large bill-posting station not far from the house where I was born, erected on the Palatine Road, a main artery leading from Manchester to the south. On this hoarding the theatres were advertised, usually in vast coloured placards, representing scenes from the latest plays, " London Successes," or popular melodrama, scenes from *The Silver King* depicting Wilson Barrett just back from Nevada in an astrakhan collar, his trilby hat raised, revealing his white hairs as he stood outside the village church listening to the hymns on Sunday. Or the poster would show us the hero bound by rope to the railway line as the 10.30 down express came roaring along—though as a fact it seemed as a rule fixed for ever in a condition of arrested animation; for truth to say, the poster artist of the period did not know the secret of the rhythmical brush.

On this alluring hoarding of many colours a plain drab-green poster was pasted every week in its own aloof position. I would watch the man with his paste-brush and bucket and step-ladder taking each fold of the poster from a bag at his side slung across his shoulders, and I wondered how he knew which sheet was the next and fitting one. But gradually the jig-saw merged into momentous intelligence. In huge block capitals was printed, at the top:

HALLÉ CONCERTS

In slightly less imposing type followed some such statement as:

"OVERTURE, ANACREON" .. Cherubini
SYMPHONY IN C MINOR .. Brahms
" TASSO " .. .. Liszt

Then, at the bottom, above a line devoted almost as an afterthought to the date and prices of tickets, a close scrutiny of the poster might discover the name

Hans Richter

Simply that and nothing more.

He was dictator of music in the North of England; and he ruled Covent Garden opera. In Manchester the young men in their heathen ignorance protested at his indifference to any composition not German or of German extraction. We petitioned the All-Father at the offices of the Hallé Concerts Society, demanding performances of modern French music. Richter dismissed us with a gruff fiat out of his whiskers; "Zer is no mod'n French musik." This was during the years of the advent of Debussy. But Richter introduced us to all the symphonic poems of Strauss in one and the same season; and old subscribers to the seats where no man dare appear except in evening dress, wrote letters to the *Manchester Guardian*, palpably crossing themselves because of the wind-machine and bleating sheep in *Don Quixote*. And *Punch* foresaw the coming of the time, not far ahead, when we would all sigh nostalgically for the good old tunes of Strauss and Debussy.

Richter also gave us Elgar. The A flat symphony is dedicated to him. Richter conducted the awful first performance of *The Dream of Gerontius* at Birmingham, where he was blamed for "a strange inability to grasp the subtleties of Elgar's thought," which is an accusation hard to support; for no conductor acquainted with *Parsifal* would be likely to find unusual modes of musical expression in *Gerontius*. The failure of *Gerontius* in Birmingham can probably be amply explained if we bear in mind the English choir of the period, and the fact that Edward Lloyd was the first Gerontius. Elgar was satisfied to trust Richter with the production of *The Apostles*, also in Birmingham, a few years later; and on the score of this work Richter inscribed the compliment, in his curious English, "Hans Richter, a true friend and an earnest admirer of the genius who had invented and scored this really original masterwork." I have often wondered what Richter "really" thought of Elgar's music.

I cannot imagine that any young man to-day will be equal to grasping the astonishing mixed state of excitement and of reverence which young men of those years felt when they knew that Elgar and Strauss and Richter were each and all actually present in their city's midst, and likely to be seen with one's own eyes any day going here or there between the Midland Hotel and Peter Street. There has been a debunking of genius and of the miraculous since then. A new work by Strauss or Elgar, like the publication of *The Dynasts* by Hardy, was an event that changed and gave higher voltage to life and to the whole world. I can feel yet the beating of my heart when Richter lifted his two arms, a little in front of him, and after a solemn roll of the drum we heard for the first time the opening phrases of the A flat symphony of Elgar, the long grave melody with the tread of bass fiddles beneath. And we knew that Elgar himself was in the audience, and that he was not as other men, but a Great man. We believed in great men then; and from afar, lurking outside the German restaurant of the Midland, or the artists' entrance of the Hallé Concerts, we worshipped them; and boasted we had seen Shelley plain.

And next day, the eagerness to read what the *Guardian* thought of it; a huge column by Langford to digest before the hour's argument in Lyon's café between one and two o'clock over coffee. I can remember reading "S.L.'s" notice of the A flat symphony and scarcely understanding a word of it:

> ". . . the work sounded peculiarly composite. The controlling theme is something adapted from the symphonic-poem to the symphony, though of course Cesar Franck has already made use of this method. The triumphant method of the final movement is that of Liszt; the symphonic development has the sinew of Brahms. The exultation and main force of the brass writing tells us of Richard Strauss. Yet with all these things we feel they are borrowed as quite legitimate technical aids, and are transformed into the composer's own being. The slow movement has a spiritual emulation of the D major section of the Choral symphony . . . Elgar has obviously written in a spirit of devout culture."

The *Guardian* never considered its readers' cultural or intellectual limitations; and what is more, none of us, even amongst its most uninformed young readers, expected "S.L." to go out of his way to accommodate us. If we didn't understand him, if he wrote above our heads, very well; we never dreamed that he should come down to our level; it was our job and duty to educate ourselves up to him.

Young men to-day cannot be expected (maybe I have written this sentence already in my book, and maybe I'll write it again) to realise how Elgar loomed on us in England in the early nineteen-hundreds. It was a dawn which " came up like thunder " ; it was a discovery that musically we did not actually dwell in a parochial island surrounded by academy professors and cantata but at last in the European stream and traffic. *Gerontius*, a failure at its first English performance, was hailed as a masterpiece at Düsseldorf, by none other than Richard Strauss. We didn't understand then that it was natural enough that the music of *Gerontius* should be easier to grasp by Germans than by English ears which had not yet heard *Parsifal*. This is not to belittle *Gerontius* as an original work. Creative genius has little to do with invention and innovation ; only in an established language can masterpieces be written at all. Elgar spoke in music he had learned to think in as inevitably as his lungs had learned to breathe ; the originality of *Gerontius* is the only kind that matters in the arts, originality of personal imaginative experience. *Gerontius* is not just a composition but the spiritual experiences of a man who dwelt seriously on the problems of life, death and the hereafter. And the religious significance of *Gerontius* is absorbed into dramatic presentation. To feel the poignancy of the music it is not more necessary to be a Catholic than it is necessary to believe in witches and ghosts to have the mind filled with the grandeur and terror of *Macbeth*. Often I have listened to *Gerontius* in the cathedrals of the West of England ;

and at the end, after " Softly and gently, dearly ransomed soul, In my most loving arms I now enfold thee . . . Swiftly shall pass thy night of trial here, And I shall come and wake thee on the morrow "—these words to music of a hushed peace that seemed there and then to ease all human hurt and apprehension; and I have scarcely been able to see in front of me because of mist of tears. But I have been aware of, sitting next me, many a gaitered divine, apparently unaffected; and I am what an orthodox Christian would call an unbeliever.

The discovery of *Gerontius*, not all at once but after repeated performances, and helped in our appreciation of it by the writings of Arthur Johnstone, Langford's predecessor on the " M.G.," and by Ernest Newman, was an event in our lives which to-day I can only liken to the mental and emotional stress excited at the present time by the advent of the atomic bomb. Every presentation of the work was more shattering than the last; and this has been my experience of the work always.

I am certain there has been no more moving Gerontius than that of Gervase Elwes; none more consuming than that of John Coates; none more heart-piercing than that of Steuart Wilson; none more human than that of Heddle Nash. In 1938, at the Albert Hall, Malcolm Sargent conducted *Gerontius*, with Nash, Gladys Ripley and Harold Williams the soloists. Even the hard-boiled London critics were snuffling at the end; and Toscanini, who had been in the audience, rushed round to the artists' room and embraced Sargent and called the work a masterpiece and, probably, wondered why he had until then not known of its existence. For strange to say, the Continent of Europe never heard of *Gerontius* after Julius Buths and Ludwig Wüllner revealed its genius to the musicians at the Lower Rhine Festival in 1902.

After almost a lifetime's knowledge of *Gerontius* and after outgrowing many technical points in it that were " new " forty years ago, and after keeping pace with the startling changes in music since Stravinsky, Bartok and Schönberg began the new " orientation," I still count it one of those few musical works of which we can say that they put us through an experience and are more than matters of art. Only in terms of inspiration (whatever is the psychological state denoted by the word) can we account for the stupendous effect on us when we hear the blaze of C major at " Praise to the Holiest." We have heard echoes of it already as from afar; and now the whole choir, voices pitched high, seem to open a great door upon a place of light. And no musical *invention*—not even musical invention of genius—could give us the transition to the second part. *Gerontius* takes us through the two worlds of man's finite doubt and torment and man's infinite trustfulness and felicity. Yet the two worlds are seen and presented with such a particularity of vision that we are able to feel the heavy feverish sick chamber, feel the terror and the chill at heart; we can hear the " emptying out of each constituent and natural force." Then, with the beginning of Part II, we hear suddenly the music or quietude of a celestial sphere—" I went to sleep, and now I am refreshed "; the soft strains suggest a harmony going on beyond Time and Space. I am always prepared to swear that this second part of *Gerontius* never actually begins; Elgar seems gently to lift a veil. The musician who is interested in origins might compare *Gerontius* at the beginning of part II with the little "Slumber" movement in the "Wand of Youth."

They say Elgar couldn't set words to music without abuse or unsubtlety of accentuation. Where, even in Hugo Wolf, is there a more apt or beautiful stress than Elgar's, on "wished" in the Angel's phrase: "You cannot now cherish a wish which ought not to be wished"? Where is there a more perfect semi-colon in all vocal music than the pause at "one moment" when the Angel sings, "Yes, for one moment thou shalt see thy Lord."

Elgar, Shaw, Wells, Ibsen, Nietzsche, Strauss, Debussy, the French Impressionists; our first tastes of Stendhal, the de Goncourts, J-K Huysmans—these last were rather late reaching England, or at any rate, Manchester; then, before our sight had become accustomed to the fresh vista, the Russians swept down on us—Dostoevsky, Turgenev, Tchekov, Moussorgsky, Rimsky-Korsakov, and the ballet. It was a renaissance; the twentieth century opened on a full and flowing sea; thus we emerged from the Victorian Age.

There were not enough hours to the day for a young man. We never went straight home after a new play by Shaw, after *Gerontius*, after the A flat symphony, after Kreisler had played the Elgar violin concerto for the first time, after *Tristan*, after Strauss's *Salome* with Aino Akté in it. We walked the city streets; we talked and talked. I begrudged sleep. Sometimes I would climb stealthily to my attic, on tiptoe for fear of waking the household and revealing the enormity of my dissipations; and I would enter my bedroom and see the furniture taking outline at break of day, the smooth untouched sheets and pillow. An hour or two afterwards, I would have to get up to go to the office where I worked as an insurance clerk. Every summer night a group of us met outside the gates of Alexandra Park, and there we talked and argued, not to air our economic grievances, not to "spout" politics and discontent, but to relieve the ferment of our minds or emotions after the impact of *Man and Superman*, *Elektra*, *Riders to the Sea*, *Pélleas and Mélisande*, *Scheherezade*, *Prince Igor*. In winter months a table was reserved for us in a Lyon's café in Albert Square; comfort and consideration were observed even in "chain" eating-houses thirty years ago. There was a warm carpet on the floor, and a coal fire glowed next to my chair at this table. I often hit my skull when I threw back my head, laughing, against the marble slab of the mantlepiece. Our waitress was Annie, a rosy-cheeked girl who never omitted to refer to us as "Mr. This," or "Mr. That." At six o'clock in the evening we assembled in Lyon's for "tea," the major meal of the day, usually two poached eggs on toast and a pot of tea, sixpence. Never have I since enjoyed food and drink with such relish—ah, the satisfaction of the first pipe—Edgeworth tobacco—while the taste of Lyon's tea remained on the palate. Then the talk; it would go on until closing time, round about nine o'clock. On Saturdays the session sometimes began at noon, if no matinée called for attention, and continued till dusk; lunch and tea, comprising much the same items from the menu, perhaps a welsh rarebit and coffee instead of poached eggs and tea, merged imperceptibly. Time in fact stood still. On the way to these heavenly gatherings I could not travel through the city fast enough; I would chafe at every halt caused by a traffic block as I raced through the thoroughfares. Usually we went into conversation with our arguments and views well prepared, and all our "quotations" carefully rehearsed; but the idea was to seem to bring them in spontaneously—with a slip made on purpose.

There was W. and his younger brother E. W. was a sort of partner in a small chemical agency; he looked in at the office to sign cheques, but for the most part he apparently spent the whole day at this table by the fireside at Lyon's. I cannot recall ever once arriving there not forestalled by W., whom we called Tom: good looking, thirty years old, supposed by the younger of our company to be a man of the world, well-dressed in grey flannel and very free with his money. He spoke plausibly, and it was suspected that he didn't know or hadn't read the half of what formed the subject and occasions of his suave discourses. He was the despair of his brother, whom I can liken only to some young eagerheart out of a George Meredith novel, as he absorbed Meredith until he suggested in every gesture and accent Richard Feveril and Harry Richmond rolled together. Tom would affect to decry Meredith compared to Hardy. "The Tragic muse," he would say, "sees deeper into life than the Comic muse. Take a noble play like *King Lear* . . ." Or just as likely it would be "Take a noble play like the *Œdipus Rex*." He once staggered us by going so far as "Take a noble play by Lope de Vegas." And his brother, Edgar by name, would go white, hold his breath very long, and when Tom's disquisition had come to a pause, would say: "Christ. Hardy's a yokel; how can you make modern literature out of bumpkins and primitive emotions? Why, there's more fundamental brainstuff in the first chapter of *The Egoist* than in the whole of Hardy put together. And what about Falstaff and Molière, if it comes to arguments about tragedy and comedy? Why, even *Hamlet* is irony as much as it is tragedy." And Tom would reply: "Take a noble play like *When We Dead Awaken*."

There was Bobbie Burns, with a game-leg, whose attempts to drag Karl Marx into our æsthetics were severely suppressed; he subscribed to Orage's paper, *The New Age*, and maybe he was one of the first of living Englishmen to throw the word *bourgeois* about amongst the masterpieces, not excepting a noble play by Calderon. He regarded Robert Blatchford a great Thinker; and one day scored heavily when he casually tossed the name of Max Stirner at us, the philosophy of Egoism, "no world but my world; no truth but my truth"—though how Bobby reconciled Stirner with the socialism of Keir Hardie he didn't explain; and to our credit, let it be said, we didn't expect it of him.

Without knowing it, we were wise to talk and contend not to prove an abstract æsthetic theory but to show off our " experiences " in books, the theatre, and music. We did not debunk with intent. Often after a maelstrom of words and quotations Tom and his brother would affect a compromise. " An exaggeration in the stress of debate, old chap. Of course I admit the genius of Meredith. . . ." " No, Tom ; you were right up to a point ; I *insist* you were right." It was all so fine and unpriggish. We were not a clique. We vied in our passionate discoveries, one against the other ; really it was an adolescent enthusiasm, in which we worshipped our Shaw and Wells and Strauss and Debussy and Meredith and Hardy and Dostoevsky much in the same way that a year or two earlier we had worshipped our Maclaren, our Fry and our Ranjitsinhji.

Every one of us would have suffered surprise and indignation if we had been told that the Manchester of these years was, for all its stir of music and theatre and ideas, a city in the English provinces, where *Tristan und Isolde* was only just impinging on a large number of minds nearly half a century after the date of its composition ; where Strauss's " Also sprach Zarathustra," composed in 1896, was causing embittered controversy by reason of its " modernity " in 1910. But London itself was also provincial then ; and we gloated at our table in the Lyon's café when Elgar in a public speech declared that the music centre of the country was situated " farther North." And Miss Horniman's Gaiety Theatre was in full swing. Busoni played one Thursday night in Manchester, only a few yards from the stage on which Sudermann's *Magda* was being acted ; and after he had finished the E flat concerto of Beethoven we left the shilling standing-places of the Free Trade Hall and saw the last act of *Magda* from the gallery of the Gaiety Theatre. Duse's part was acted by a good replica, a Miss Darragh—nobody ever heard of her baptism name; she was pale and plain, and could stand still saying nothing while what was being spoken by other characters, something revealed to her for the first time, caused her face to take on new traces of realisation ; she seemed to age.

Not all the finest artists become known to the world at large. Many circumstances, which have nothing to do with art, are frequently needed to make extraordinary talent and subtlety of imagination known to the many. In the days of the Beecham opera we in Manchester knew that one of the greatest living actors in opera was Frank Mullings ; I call him an actor because his voice, a tenor, was often strangled by unnatural production, yet it was the most histrionic voice I have heard amongst all the tenors known or suffered by me ; and as a creator of character, or rather, as an artist with power to incarnate a dramatic conception, I have known only one in opera who was his superior, and that Chaliapine. He was a noble towering presence as Othello. When he told the quarrellers to put up their swords, with superb implication of his shame for them, what loftiness and unself-conscious dignity of carriage ! When he appeared in the closing scene, to kill Desdemona, his intense silence—he could fill the theatre with intense silence—the torment of his awareness to what he was about to do, the sense that he knew he was caught in the snare of his own blood and passion; it was all much more than great art. This was "the pity of it"; we were taken up into a realisation of the tragically entangled texture of being. I have been told that when he entered the bedroom of Desdemona with a quietness that was as a sleep-walker's, the artist playing Desdemona often was really apprehensive that Mullings might forget himself and stray beyond histrionics into actuality. His collapse to the earth at the end of the scene in the hall of the castle was a subsidence in nature; we had seen simple manliness and trustfulness suffer corruption. Mullings never let us forget that Othello was compact of primitive stuffs not easily jealous but, being wrought, perplex'd in the extreme. Mullings, in fact, was the only artist I have known who, throughout the opera, kept us constantly reminded that Othello, after all, is Shakespeare's and not Verdi's creation.

So with his Tristan, never heard of in Bayreuth or the Metropolitan. Much of quality in the world does indeed go by and the crowd never hears of it. I have seen most of the celebrated Tristans of the last thirty years. I have heard the music sung with a vocal splendour far beyond the best in Mullings's command; but nobody has by voice and *presence* made me feel, with the intensity of Mullings, the inmost heart and mind of Tristan, and, much more important, the tragic doom that invisibly follows him about. At his entrance in Act I, when Tristan at the request of Isolde comes through the curtain of Isolde's parlour on the deck of the ship, he brought with him poignantly tragic foreknowledge; he was the music embodied. The *lento* theme in the strings, with the heavy and bodeful accents, has never been so " lived up to " as when Mullings stood facing Isolde, and in tones achingly toneless said, " Demand, lady, what you will."

In the second act, during the love-duet, his voice actually lent tragic eloquence to the music by very reason of its hint of uncertainty of pitch ; the strict ear was sometimes lacerated but somehow it was absolutely right. I once whispered to Langford in the darkened theatre, " He's out of tune, worse than ever," and Langford grunted back, " So's Wagner ! " The fever and delirium of Act III consumed him ; Mullings was an enormous man in physique, yet as we saw this Tristan raving and heaving on his pallet, we could swear he was being wasted before our very eyes. Nobody has melted, as Mullings melted, when Tristan, full to overflowing in the heart, clasped the old servitor and cried out, " O Kurwenal, du trauter Freund ! " As Parsifal he stood watching the ritual of the unfolding of the Grail as nobody else. Other tenors might as well leave the stage ; perhaps they most of them do leave it—I have never, so to say, " checked-up " on them. Mullings did not allow us to forget his presence, though he was concealed in the darkness. By some power of histrionic suggestion we could see through the eyes of Parsifal as well as through our own ; and so the drama was heightened to a spiritual dualism ; we suffered the agony of Amfortas ; and at the same time we were moved by the innocence of Parsifal.

Mullings ennobled everything ; the second-rate assumed a sense of imaginative largeness and dignity if

Mullings touched it. Even in the dreadful opera of Saint-Saëns, heroic pathos stood before us when Mullings was led into the temple, the blind Samson, by the little boy. When he stood between two pillars (obvious "props") and outstretched his arms, we could feel the gathering of enormous power in a deliberate weighing of effort; the theatre entire might well have come crashing down. In the experience and vision of art it did. It was the spell cast by the sincerity of Mullings that persuaded some of us once on a time to believe the songs of Bantock, "Ferishtah's Fancies", were comparable to Wolf's for psychological insight and rightness of emotional expression. It was, of course, his incomparable enunciation of Browning's poetry (though I am not saying that the songs themselves do not contain strokes of musical talent and are neglected to-day in favour of inferior stuffs); I have heard no singer give to English words the imaginative point, salience and voltage of Mullings. Words seemed to be alive as they came from his mouth; the accent was poignant and intensely savoured. And so, no doubt, the music of Bantock was warmed by this diction of Mullings, as invisible writing comes into significant and palpable meaning from contact with heat. I can always hear him, in a tone not of the present but reaching towards some dim uncertain futurity, not merely singing but questioning, in the intonation of pure poetry:

Only, at the heart's utmost joy and triumph, terror
Sudden turns the blood to ice: a chill wind disencharms
All the late enchantment! What if all be error——

He would achieve a mezza-voce and pronounce " error " in two syllables, vanishing to silence. Like Chaliapine he could play the fool, bestrew the stage with a wreckage of horse-play, rubicund and somehow bacchantic. As Canio in *Pagliacci* he reduced all other singers of the part to the silliest Italian operatics, not excepting Caruso, by the tragic gusto he generated. When he discovered Nedda and Silvio together we could understand why Silvio fled for his life. He would seize Nedda and send her spinning to the boards ; he once *threw* Desirée Ellinger right off the stage into the wings. And nobody has invited a crowd of yokels to the show with the allurement of Mullings, emphasing each of his points in his advertisement with a drumstick that spoke the subtlest shades of emphasis. Tears have come into my eyes to hear Mullings sing the old song, " Have you seen but a white lily ? " he caressed the word " smutch'd " so that you would see and feel the softness and the texture of loveliness. He was an artist in a thousand, and the North of England knew it, not only the masses that packed the Beecham opera seasons in Quay Street, Manchester, but one or two of the discerning minds of the day—Newman, Langford, not to mention Beecham himself. The world in general that has raved over performers on the larynx in La Scala and the Metropolitan have never heard of Mullings ; I for one, who believe that the rarest of the pleasures of life should be preserved by a few, do not deplore it.

I have enjoyed Toscanini's impeccable conducting of *Falstaff* at Salzburg, with Stabile in the cast ; it is not to be remembered for a day by anybody who remembers the sparkle, the champagne cup, of the Beecham ensemble in *Falstaff*. This may seem a tall saying but I am satisfied it is true; true, at any rate for me.

For three months in the year the Beecham seasons filled the largest of Manchester's theatres, and amongst the artists were the best ever known in English opera—Ranalow, Radford (perfect as the Father in *Louise*), Walter Hyde, Percy Heming, Maurice D'Oisley, Frederick Austin, Edna Thornton, Kirkby Lunn, Mignon Nevada, John Coates, Sylvia Nelis, Rosina Buckman, to name a few. Buckman's "Butterfly" was exquisite; she was a vast size but nobody noticed it. Her voice was none other than the heart and every impulse of Cho-Cho-San; she sang the part on the scale of miniature pathos; and those who never heard Buckman asking Sharpless to read the letter, those who have never heard her tell him of the season of the year when the robins built their nests; who never heard her tone, intolerably trustful when she asked Suzuki to put a little carmine on her cheeks, have never heard the opera transformed from La Scala, Covent Garden and the Metropolitan into a pathetic world in which Butterfly, a pretty figure from a Japanese fan, is caught in the trap of circumstance incomprehensible to her in its tragic hurtfulness. At least they have not heard it, and not heard many other delights, with the enchanted ears of young men who hung on to every note in the Quay Street theatre in Manchester years ago, from our congested places, first on one foot then the other, jammed in pit alcoves at the back, or straddling on the stairs of the high circle, while Beecham, whom we likened to a wizard over a cauldron of orchestral charms in the dark theatre, wafted into our senses the magic from his baton.

Sometimes in the summer months, when I was engaged as cricket-coach at Shrewsbury School, I would steal away and catch the half-past four train in the afternoon to Manchester, to get there for the rising of the curtain at the Beecham opera. I would wait till all the house-matches were in full swing, the field flashing white and green in the sun. I was supposed to keep an eye on form. With a feeling of awful secrecy I would glide imperceptibly from the scene, race along the High Street, get to Shrewsbury railway station with not a moment in hand. I suffered curious apprehension; perhaps the train might be wrecked. There were many miles to cover before the striking of the enchanted hour and the reaching of the enchanted place in Quay Street. In all the manifold complications of a train and a railway it was easy for a single screw or bolt to get loose in the entrails of the engine, or amongst the steel and woodwork of the permanent way. The hours were leaden; to get as far as Crewe was a rack of frustration. And when at last I reached London Road, Manchester, I did not wait to take a taxi; I believed I could defeat time and space better by volitional energy, by running as fast as I could; and in those days I could run like the wind. Across the city, short cuts through back streets quietening down after the day's work, lined with warehouses redolent of grey cloth—through these devious ways I would race, scattering stray cats, outraging occasional pedestrians round street corners; and with a heart thumping like a battering-ram I obtained my seat, and while the sweat was still wet on my forehead I heard the chords of the overture of *Meistersinger* crash out and the music unfold like a banner to the sustained half-close, then the wonderful modulation at the rise of the curtain to the chorale in St. Katharine's :

Da zu dir der Heiland kam.

At midnight I returned to Shrewsbury, arriving there before dawn ; and I would walk along the narrow twisting streets, timbered buildings, silent under the midsummer moon. The Nürnberg scene came to life, while the music still was a warm flood in the whole of my being. I expected to hear the horn of the Night Watchman. The scent of the lilac was wafted from the avenue near the River Severn as I climbed the stairs and entered my bedroom while the first twittering of birds came from under the eaves. And I would see the book I had left on my pillow, hours or æons ago before I had left my lodgings, without a word to a soul, and had stolen away, and absented myself from one felicity for another.

· VI ·

WHEN I was a boy and grew a little less shy I drifted into company which was probably deplorable. My companions lacked civilisation; none of them wished to get on in the way of decent citizenship. Their private ambitions in life would doubtless have lured them to reprehensible ends if education and environment had not in time overwhelmed most of them into respectability. There was Johnny Howard, for example; he set his heart on piracy in the China Seas; he once actually ran from home but was found three miles distant by the police, and brought back clinging to every iron rail on the way. In later years he settled down as clerk in the employment of an old-established "Manchester house" with connections in the Far East. He rose to head clerk, and I saw him only a year or two ago, sitting in the same small office at the same desk. He was still thin and unkempt but now grey; he wore eye-glasses and a stiff winged collar and was not unwilling to tell me that he'd been there thirty-five years man and boy, never missing a day, never once arriving a minute later than nine o'clock, always taking his lunch in the old place, the Kardomah café downstairs, a cup of coffee and sardines on toast; and going home to Didsbury on the five-fifty. In the course of years fortune divided us ; I travelled as far from Portland Street, where John worked, as Australia ; and when I came back, chance carried me past this famous " Manchester house," and I looked in for old time's sake ; and there he was, seated in the tiny office, a circular glow of electricity coming from under a green shade ; an old dusty pot of gum on the mantelpiece in exactly the same place where it had stood when last I had called. I had crossed the equator, and a thousand golden hours had fallen in the hour-glass ; and John had been here all the time, patient, industrious, and happy enough.

There were Billy Clegg and Harry Pinkerton and Herbert Ramsbottom. Not one of them coveted his neighbour's wife nor his house nor his ox. Not one of them dreamed of the day when he would rise as chairman and address a shareholders' meeting and announce a prosperous year. We hated the very idea of what the world called work ; we didn't want wealth or whisky-and-sodas or a villa in the suburbs. If Billy Clegg prayed every night that he would one day be chosen as Manchester City's outside-left it was not fame that he thought of but the glory of speeding along the wing, his feet twinkling, while a crowd of Manchester lads roared him on familiarly. As a matter of gospel fact, Billy actually did play for Manchester City. There has never been his equal in his position. He was small and bow-legged, and chewed a toothpick as he waited for the ball. When it was passed to him and it fell at his feet he would " trap " it and lever it to an inch of where he wanted it, as though invisible prongs or feelers had emanated suddenly from his toes; then off he went, down the field, dribbling they called it in those days; it was not then considered necessary that a great player should get rid of the ball as soon as it came to him. Like the wind Billy ran, or like a light he flickered, with feints this way and that, to thwart and get round a thudding and charging opponent. It seemed that he left behind him a litter of bodies picking themselves up bovinely, hardly knowing in which direction to look for Billy, towards which goal. I think Billy once won a Cup Final by scoring from the touchline; but I am not sure.

We did not read crime stories; our literature seldom descended to common burglars or forgers or murderers. Raffles was a gentleman cracksman. So Harry Pinkerton set his heart on a haul on a dazzling scale in Hatton Gardens; in his spare time he proposed to play for Middlesex. Herbert Ramsbottom's ambition was peculiar —to own one of those "Try your strength" things at a fair which you hit with a mallet, sending a metal object upwards along a slot to ring a bell, or rather just not to ring it.

We called ourselves (of course) "The Gang," and roamed the streets, but not with intent to despoil or disturb peace in a large or heinous way. At our worst we would tie street door-knobs together, then knock, and watch results from a hidden refuge. Or we would open milk-cans standing in porches on rainy mornings on our way to school; or in various improvised disguises ask the same old gentleman the time of day. Altogether our gangsterism was a kind of art for art's sake, interesting to nobody but ourselves. We swore sepulchrally to remain loyal until death, not to any specific programme or person—just a general or universal loyalty. On one point only did our oath go into detail; any member of the "Gang" who "spooned" with a girl was expelled—no, "exiled" was the penalty—for life.

Most of us lived in back streets, and at any moment a virago in a shawl would appear at a doorway, and after a swift comprehensive glance right and left, a penetrating voice would cry out "'Arry! Come in and fetch coal oop!" As a rule the "Gang" conducted its operations well beyond the view and reach of home. It was all a game of make-believe. We could not even play cricket without histrionics. On the day at Leeds when Johnny Briggs fell into a fit while playing for England against Australia, we were engaged on a melancholy waste of land, also enacting a Test match in miniature (or replica). An excited urchin, Sammy Ogden, a little late into action that evening, came tearing over the earth even as I was setting my field in the character and gestures of A. C. Maclaren; and my "long-stop" was the youngest of the Moffitts next door, who wasn't really qualified yet for big cricket because he reached hardly as high as the wickets. With the awful tidings from Leeds hot in his mouth, Sammy Ogden appeared upon us like a messenger in a Greek play. "What's the matter?" we asked. And, again like a messenger in a Greek play, he broke into blank verse:

Briggs 'e's gone and 'ad a fit at Leeds,
Taken off the field 'e wos to-day;
And England now can only bat ten men.

Messenger Ogden's news heightened the drama of our own Test match in the dusty sunshine of that hot summer. The youngest Moffitt immediately acted Johnny Briggs having a fit; and as Maclaren (myself) and the eldest Moffitt (Joe Darling the Australian captain) led him off the field he made spit in his mouth to represent foam.

No games-master would have approved of our monkeyings; even at cricket we were without ambition that went beyond our own romantic conceits. On one evening the elder Moffitt would take a long strenuous rather unrhythmical run and would bowl fast because of some inspiration from Tom Richardson in the day's news; a week later he would probably moderate his pace to very slow, and his approach to the wicket would decline to a few strides—his idol now being Wilfred Rhodes. Herbert Ramsbottom might be seen crossing his legs and trying a glance. "Ranjisinhji," he would say laconically. We played games amongst ourselves, "picked sides," as we called it, and tossed for innings by throwing into the air an old war-scarred bat and shouting "Flat!" or "Round!" There was nobody to score for us; each batsman was trusted to keep count of the runs he himself made, which put an inordinate strain upon his honesty. The wicket-keeper held a coat before him to stop the byes and he would throw it at a wide. Also there were no umpires; in cases of disputes a majority vote was called. If the vote proved indecisive we fell back on arbitrament by force. Possession of the bat was nine points of our law, when it came to the pinch; the batsman must not "give it up." The game frequently digressed into a tug-of-war.

Yet there was method in our licentiousness. We aped the contemporary heroes of cricket and declined to study technique in the abstract, but none of us could pretend to be J. T. Hearne without some show of an off-break. The boy who posed as Johnny Tyldesley was obliged to execute a square-cut as a sort of "make-up," to lend an air of verisimilitude. The "Gang" was the nursery of no fewer than two county players and a professional cricket coach; those who can—do; those who cannot—teach. In all, I can count four or five of the untrained, uneducated street-roaming companions of my youth who eluded respectable instruction and drifted into occupations of romance and joy in the theatre, sport, journalism, literature. One of them even distinguished himself in some office of public utility. And nothing of utility, public or otherwise, was taught at the school we attended; no classes or essays in social welfare, hygiene and what not. The idea of an essay put into our darkened brains usually began this way: "I am a pencil; my grandfather was a tree in a forest."

It was Eric Brindley who opened my eyes to certain cultural limitations latent in the "Gang" and their activities. In any case, schism was setting in, that disintegration to which all human institutions must submit sooner or later. Eric never really belonged to the "Gang"; he was only an hon. member, so to say; he lived in a semi-detached house with bay-windows, and his father was "in the city". Eric went to the Grammar School, wore his white Eton collar over his jacket, not under it, and never nailed Blakey's Protectors into the soles and heels of his boots. He introduced me to the school stories of Talbot Baines Reed; and he became my hero and Dux, though he was only my senior by a year. He called his father and mother pater and mater. We went about arm-in-arm calling one another silly asses and using our surnames freely. He was the best boy batsman I have ever known, and our friendship received its seal one Saturday afternoon when Eric was playing for the same boys' club as myself in the summer holidays. We scored a hundred runs together in a partnership which won the match after all had seemed lost beyond repair. In course of time Eric took me home with him, by way of the back kitchen to begin with, on evenings when their "general help" was having her night off. After a while Eric introduced me to the family, and I was led to the drawing-room situated upstairs, my first glimpse into the English middle-classes. There was a grand piano in the corner, my first sight of one at close quarters. Bookcases with glass windows, a huge picture in a gold frame in the Italian manner, and a good deal of drapery and plush. Mr. Brindley was handsome (an older Eric), grey towsled hair and a moustache like Sir Charles Bancroft. His manner was very spacious and I thought his eyes seemed a little watery. He combined impatience with robustiousness and friendliness of manner. At once he called me "me boy." Mrs. Brindley was small and motherly to everybody. The elder son, perhaps one of the first avowed highbrows in the history of English intellectual development of the nineteen-hundreds, also worked in the city but did not look like it at home. He was very severe, with wing-collar and views about Shaw, Ibsen and the Fabian Essays. But the first thing I remember about Mr. Brindley is the casual way, without interrupting his talk, he squirted a syphon into a glass of whisky.

One day Eric asked me, on behalf of his father, to come to dinner; and it was to take place in the evening. Until now my notions of dinner was a joint on Sundays at half-past twelve. So I arrived at Eric's house after dark, neatly attired in a clean collar like Eric's, polished boots, and my hair plastered down with water. There was a dining-room downstairs, and the table had no cloth on it. Plates and knives and forks and spoons were arranged in symmetrical order on polished wood. Tablecloths so far had been a source of anxiety at all dinner times; my grandmother never served me without saying, "Now don't mess t' tablecloth." Mr. Brindley and the elder son wore evening clothes, and Mrs. Brindley and the daughter Cecilia were splendid in black velvet and lace. Cecilia was, I thought, very pretty. A stout woman, red in the face but spick and span in her apron, served the soup. There was a battery of cutlery at the side of my plate, so I waited for the others to begin. Suddenly Mr. Brindley bent his head and said a grace. "For what we are about to consume let us render thanks to whatever gods there be." Wine was drunk, and Mr. Brindley pronounced it champagne in the French way, as I subsequently learned. He poured a little of it into my glass but I did not dare. Eric drank as though unafraid; and he was not yet fifteen. "A boy should learn to take his liquor like a gentleman," said Mr. Brindley.

I recollect little more of this, my first experience of dining-out. I did not go often into the Brindley's inner circle, but Eric and I enjoyed the kitchen and his little " den," where he possessed a bookshelf and a writing-desk.

Not long afterwards, scarcely a year if I am not mistaken, Mr. Brindley became an invalid and seldom was seen outside his house. On a New Year's Eve I was taken by Eric upstairs to the drawing-room again. Mr. Brindley sat swathed in a dressing-gown and flannel and shawl. A little stool by the side of him held a medicine bottle and glasses. He shook hands with me, rising from his chair like Lazarus. He looked more distinguished and blown than ever. He took an interest in my attempts to be a writer. Eric, he said, was destined for the law. He gave me advice, in measured accents. " The adjective is the enemy of the noun, never forget it, me boy." " The fewest words in the simplest order." " Easy writing, hard reading." He showed me a cuttings-book containing many letters from him to the Editor of the *Manchester Guardian* on various topics political and theatrical, including one arguing against Tariff Reform, signed " Economist."

He would cast his eyes upwards, showing the whites, and go off at a tangent into monologues about the past. " Enchanting. Enchanting. Hic olim. . . ." He defended C. P. Scott and his attitude to the Boer War. " A blot on the 'scutcheon of England. Never live it down." He despised Kipling. " Banjo doggerel." The day of

Imperialism was done too. Religion of Humanity, and Comte, and Frederic Harrison. Without warning he rose from his chair, and in a voice that was like the sound of the sea, he recited:

For thee, O now a silent soul, my brother,
Take at my hands this garland, and farewell.
Thin is the leaf, and chill the wintry smell,
And chill the solemn earth, a fatal mother,
With sadder than the Niobean womb.
And in the hollow of her breasts a tomb.
Content thee, howsoe'er, whose days are done;
There lies not any troublous thing before,
Nor sight nor sound to war against thee more
For whom all winds are quiet as the sun,
All waters as the shore.

My introduction to Swinburne. And then the New Year was greeted. Champagne once more, with linked hands and Mr. Brindley leading the old song:

We'll tak' a cup of kindness yet
For Auld Lang Syne.

It could not have been long after this New Year's Eve that I went with Eric on an errand to a Manchester provision dealer's, called an "Italian Warehouseman." The man behind the counter looked at the order list, then went away to speak to somebody. When he returned he gave Eric a note, asking him to deliver it to Mrs. Brindley. That year there was an auction sale in

Laburnum Terrace. Strange folk clumped up and down the stairs. Chairs and tables and sideboards were carried into the street, where for a while they stood exposed to the public view before they were carted off to unknown destinations, the grand piano with them. I never saw Eric again ; the family disappeared.

Not a story to recollect in such a book as this, you may ask, or in such a chapter, you may think? My justification is that the occurrence taught me ironic appreciation, without which few pleasures can be called back at all without insipidity. Besides, I can record a happy ending, or at any rate an ending to Eric which keeps his place secure amongst those companions of my boyhood who escaped the commonplace and dowdy end. Eric reappeared in the Far East and married a lovely girl born there. Also he contrived to score a brilliant century in a first-class match against a strong English team on tour, passing that way.

I have never been interested in sport as such ; I am not appealed to by the excitement or speculation of games. Except during Lancashire and Yorkshire matches at cricket I have not cared about wins and losses. I would rather see one of my best off-breaks hit to the boundary than bowl a man out with a long-hop. My love of cricket has little to do with the sportsman's instincts ; as a fact, I am bored by most indoor or open-air "pastimes," and by those people who play them. Card-players I have found usually to be actual or potential bores. Tennis cannot possibly be a great game because women have been known to attain proficiency at it. Golf is really sedentary middle-aged ; and though football has the greatness which comes into any activity that exposes a man to physical hurt, it is for me too actively combative, with none of the lazy irrelevances of cricket. Still, I like at times to watch a football match because of the crowd. A game's greatness is determined by the variety of human nature looking on. I once saw Manchester City playing Sheffield United before an enormous multitude. A brilliant piece of footwork was performed by the centre half-back, and a Sheffield man standing next to me in a muffler and a cloth cap said, simply and laconically, to one and all within the vicinity, " Finesse ! " It was to be doubted whether any ordinary occasion or occurrence in life would have prompted this man to the use of such a word.

I like to hear a crowd cheering a footballer along as he races down the field, a few doubting Thomases snarling " Get rid of it ; get rid of it ! " I have seen a famous centre-forward leave his opposition helplessly in his rear, with no suspicion of ever being offside. The roars of many voices swell to a crescendo, in which expectation, admiration and anxiety are poignantly mixed. " Look at 'im—a bobby-dazzler ! Shoot ! Shoot ! Shoot, you bloody fool ! " I have seen this centre-forward, with an open goal before him ; and he has missed—sent the ball skimming over the crossbar by feet. And twenty thousand throats a moment ago choiring like the cherubim and all the sons of joy, have changed to execration. Except the sceptic who is always there, ready to say he told you so. " 'E never wos class ;

temperamental, that's wot 'e is. Always 'as been." The same centre-forward has on this very afternoon, a few moments later, scored a magnificent goal, into the corner of the net, the ball a thud of cannon, the goal-keeper prone on the muddy earth and, apparently, *seconds* late. And the same doubting Thomas, without shame and in a louder voice than before, has shouted to the whole world, "Best bloody centre-forward in England. Or bloody well Scotland, if it comes to that. Always said so, *years* ago when he played for Tranmere Rovers. Wants feedin', that's all. Wants the ball, that's all. Always said so."

Without a great crowd no great game. And men must predominate, and what is more, it must be largely composed of what once on a time was called the working-classes. Saturday noon ; a pint at the pub, then dinner time, and after that, off to t' match. The gathering hosts. High on the mounds they stand, leaning against iron rail supports. A band of trumpets, euphonium or bombardon march round the field, led by somebody very straight in the back, swinging a long silver knobbed stick round and round with one hand held out full stretch. The teams run into the field from an underground corridor that slopes downward ; they are striped like zebras and they look as though they have been released into the arena. Then the preliminaries at each goal by antagonists who apparently do not notice one another, or at any rate have not yet been introduced ; next the appearance of the linesman, fussy and important, and now the referee appears, busily omnipresent. The teams arrange themselves into positions ; a centre-forward makes passes with his right toe over and round the ball, and with the gentlest flick to the wing the kick-off is performed, and the crowd's noises rise and fall like an organ and the ocean wave. The swift movements of the ball, this way and that way, yet never out of control; unseen strings pull it here and there. Suddenly there is a hiatus in the rhythm of long "passing"; a scramble, a melée on the distant left wing. The referee at once manifests himself; a minute or two ago he was in another dimension of combat. He points at the earth ferociously, and the players disentangle themselves and line-up while a corner kick is taken, in a period of suspended animation amongst the crowd.

The great game must have pageantry about it and bring forth variety of a man's nature, especially humour of national character. The crowd must take it to heart and get upset and brood during the week upon its ups and downs. It must at times lay heavily upon the minds of the people and render them gloomy. Years ago Lancashire defeated Yorkshire, in a cricket match at Leeds, a victory by some twenty runs. On the third morning Yorkshire had wanted a mere fifty to win, with all their wickets to fall. During an epic August Bank Holiday Lancashire had collapsed in a second innings, all out just before close of play; and the crowd went home content that the issue could be regarded as settled. Next day hardly anybody visited the ground, except those necessary to go through the formalities attendant upon obtaining the correct statistics of a ten-wickets victory for Yorkshire—the players, the scorers, the umpires, the press, with perhaps a handful of members as witnesses, and a few cloth caps with " nowt else to do " and anyway t' bars would be open while Sutcliffe and Holmes were knocking off t' runs.

Gentle rain in the night had made the turf capricious, and before we knew what was happening the Yorkshire innings fell into wrack and ruin. When the last batsman was overwhelmed and Lancashire had really and truly won the match, I rushed from the ground eager to carry the good news back to Manchester. I leapt on a tram, sat down inside, and the guard came with his tickets. " What's they won by—lost any wickets gettin' them ? " I told him that Lancashire, not Yorkshire, were the victors. He expressed some impatience. " Ah'm talkin' about t' cricket," he said, presumably under the impression I had come straight from a polo match or archery tournament. I repeated to him the dreadful truth, and he suspended business at once. He didn't give me a ticket but turned his back on me and walked from the almost empty tram, conveyed the news to a trolley-boy, who relayed it to the driver. The tram proceeded to travel some three miles into Leeds by its own volition.

When I reached the railway station, I was a little in advance of the departure of the train to Manchester, so I entered a refreshment-room and sat down at a little table. Shortly afterwards, a man sat down next to me, cap and muffler, and spoke in the speech of Laisterdyke. " Eh, dear," he said, " who'd a' thowt it ? Faa-ncy Yorksheer crackin' oop like that. Ah'd never a' thowt it." There was no anger in his voice, no tone of abuse directed at the faltering Yorkshire eleven. There was only the accent of sorrow. " Eh, dear," he repeated, " it's a rum 'un." He eyed me carefully, then said, " Tha doesn't seem to be takin' this very much to 'eart " ; and I was obliged to explain to him that, as I came from Lancashire and Manchester, born and bred there, I couldn't be expected to " take it to heart " exactly. He looked at me from a different angle.

" So tha'rt from Lankysheer art tha, eh, dear ; and tha's from Lankysheer ? "

" Yes, from Lancashire."

A slight pause.

" And tha's coom all way from Manchester to watch match, ast tha ? "

" Yes, that's it," I answered.

" And tha's goin' back to Manchester by two-twenty train, eh ? "

Yes, I told him, I was indeed returning to my native city by the two-twenty train. After another short spell of meditation, he said :

" Tha'll be feelin' very pleased with thisell, won't thi' ? "

" Naturally," I replied, taking care not to look too triumphant.

" Eh, by gum. Faa-ncy Yorksheer crackin' like that. Aye. Tha'll be feelin' very pleased with thisell. Ah shouldn't wonder."

And he repeated the question :

" And tha's goin' back to Manchester by two-twenty train, art tha ? "

Feeling now a little access of irritation, I answered :

"Yes, straight back."

"Well," he said, without the slightest heat, "Ah 'opes tha drops down de-ead before tha gets there."

If a game doesn't exhibit elemental character, and loosen springs of unself-conscious humour, I can find no use for it. I can remember happenings at cricket which seemed to have been devised by a great Comic Muse who very much loved the English, especially the North English people. On a certain morning in another Lancashire and Yorkshire match at Old Trafford, in 1939, the cricketer Mitchell arrived at the wicket early, and stone-walled through the afternoon. In other and less passionate matches, Mitchell was not above a brilliant stroke or two; but he reserved himself especially for Old Trafford, when the crowd, many of them liberated at Whitsun from the pits and factories, had come out to take the air and enjoy themselves. In dead silence everybody ached in resigned boredom. Maiden over followed maiden over, and Mitchell got down lower and lower over his bat. Thirty runs he made in two hours.

Suddenly the stillness was broken by a voice, weary and outraged:

"Every bloody year; every so-and-so year 'e cooms 'ere. This so-and-so Mitchell, and 'e spoils Bank 'Oliday. Every so-and-so year."

Silence again, disturbed only by the sullen and muffled bat of Mitchell. More maidens. The voice, of a man in a hard bowler hat, was raised again:

"Every bloody year, every so-and-so year." Thus far he had addressed nobody in particular; it was an apostrophe to abstract reason and justice and toleration. But now, he directed himself to the crowd around him.

" Every so-and-so bloody year 'e cooms 'ere. I said to my missus this mornin', ' Ah goin' to Owd Trafford and what's more that so-and-so Mitchell 'll stay in all bloody day, that 'e will. Every so-and-so year 'e does it, and 'e'll do it agen.' That's what Ah said to ma missus. And look at 'im ; 'ere he so-and-so bloody well is."

Another descent into a dreadful stillness. And now, the man in the hard hat spoke to Mitchell personally.

" Thee, Mitchell ! " he called out. " Ah'm talkin' to thee. Every so-and-so year tha's been coomin' 'ere spoilin' Bank 'Oliday. Every bloody year. But listen to me, Mitchell—aye Ah'm talkin' to thee and doan't pretend tha can't 'ear. Every so-and-so year tha's been muckin' up Bank 'Oliday 'ere. But Ah'll tell thi summat tha doesn't know." He took a deep breath. " There's goin' to be a so-and-so war, me lad, so tha won't bloody well be coomin' 'ere next year. Good afternoon and t' 'ell wi' thi." He gave Mitchell a last look and went home.

I haven't attended many race-meetings since I was strangely obsessed for a year by horses ; I remember Whisk Broom and Willonyx. I went to the Grand National when Willonyx won carrying ten stone seven pounds or thereabouts ; the favourite was from Ireland, named Rathnally. Everybody was persuaded to back, or as the papers expressed it, " support," Rathnally.

The horse was favourite from Land's End to John o' Groats, from Cork to Dublin.

In flashing spring sunshine Aintree was congested. "They're off!" roared the throng. And at a preliminary "jump," which any cat could have leaped across comfortably, Rathnally fell, unseated his jockey, rolled over and over, then picked himself up on his four slender legs, and began to munch the grass, snuffling here and there, at leisure, while ruin stalked the course and men looked on with reddening faces and bulging eyes.

For months—and I was not more than eighteen years old—I studied form and the reports from Newmarket by Augur, Solon, Man on the Spot, and Captain Coe. I imagined that Captain Coe (of the *Star*) resembled Joe Bagstock. I recall the comprehensive vision of these guides to the turf, as they prognosticated: "If Swallow Tail can stay the distance; on the other hand, Fishplate at Kempton Park in June conceded four pounds to Mademoiselle and won easily. Danger may come from Forcibility, while I am credibly informed that Oatmeal must not be left out of calculations. Much as I am attracted to Slightly Soiled (and we must bear in mind that this stable is in form just now), I cannot ignore recent evidence that he is a rogue. The race is unusually open but I must make my choice, and so, with respect for Forcibility, and not forgetting Parsimony's penchant for this course, I plumb for Mackerel Sky, and suggest a saver, each way, on Gunga Din." I once met the racing correspondent of one of the daily papers with twice the largest circulation in the North of England;

he called himself Persimmon; and I always thought of him as an orchidaceous man in checks, chewing a cigar, travelling inevitably by Pullman car and calling for whisky and soda by reflex action. He turned out to be quiet of disposition, dyspeptic and a family man who seldom betted. Myself, I gambled according to various systems, my stake seldom going beyond a shilling or two. I "followed" stables—Coulthwaite at Manchester, Peacock at York, Wootton at Epsom, but it was confusing to find that each trainer invariably ran two or three horses in the same race. My very first winner was chosen from the list of probable starters because I liked the animal's name—Brünnhilde. It won at fourteen to one. I picked Wotan for a Melbourne Cup on the same principle; it won at a hundred to one. I have since known several experienced racing men, and they have all agreed that my first system for discovering winners, by association values of names, or euphony, is as good as any. "I frequently adopt it myself," confessed Lord Derby. I would "plunge" to-morrow to the extent of ten shillings, each way, on any horse bearing the name of Tristan, or Hans Sachs, or even Rienzi.

One day at the Manchester races, in a November mist, I saw a man deep in thought outside the entrances to the course; he walked up and down, hands clasped behind him trailing a walking-stick. His brow was knit, and round his face was a red-spotted handkerchief tied on the top of his head. He wore no hat. Also he lacked collar, and there was a hungry look in his gaunt aspect. Abruptly he ceased his perambulations, and he began to make fierce wide semi-circles with his stick in the earth in front of him, crouching to do so; and he muttered in low tones to himself as though performing an incantation. Then he let out a wild shout. "Come 'ere." He gathered an audience by expense of strenuous physical energy, crouching and extending himself upwards, walking round and round in his semi-circle, making passes with his stick, eyes half out of his head.

"Listenterme. I'm not a tipster. See!"—(with a sudden rush of ferocity to his head)—"naow, I'm not a tipster. I'm not sellin' you hinfermation. I don't pretend to know wottle win every race terday. And wotsmore, gen'l'men, ter tell yer the truth I'm not interested in every race, just not hinterested. Can't waste me time. I'm on'y interested in the Big Race, the November 'Andicap. Thatsall *I'm* hinterested in, gen'l'men. No; I'm tellin' yer no lie but I simply doan't know wottle win the onerclock or the twoerclock. Ask 'im over there—e'll know, oh yus 'e'll tell yer." He jerked his thumb over his shoulder, indicating another of his fraternity, announcing his winners violently from the height of a ladder.

He glared at the small crowd before him, then crouched lower than ever to the ground, and took a pile of envelopes from one of the pockets of his coat. "Listenterme," he said sepulchrally, "listenterme, gen'l'men. In these envelopes I've got the nime of the winner of the November 'Andicap. Take it or leave it. It's 'ere; and it's yours for ten shillings each, and, gen'l'men, you'll keep it to yourself. Live and let live. The absolute winner—'ere, in these envelopes." Apparently the race was likely to contain several winners, but he knew the one that would really count.

" *And* I'm not givin' away styble secrets. Stybles don't give anythink away, gen'l'men. And wotsmore, I'm not the sorter feller what betr'ys a confidence. Somer the most famous trainers in England are counted amongst my friends. Listenterme. The styble wottle win this year's November 'Andicap knose wottle win it; and wotsmore, they know that I know. See? It's a Job—S.P. See?"

He fiercely shook the envelopes in our faces. " Ten shillin's! the winner of the November 'Andicap for nineteen 'undred and ite. Christ. Ten shillin's each the packet, gen'l'men. It's *givin'* it away. Ten shillin's. Jesus. It's orful. *Givin'* it away, gen'l'men."

Not a soul in the small crowd seemed impressed. So he dug a deeper semi-circle in the earth in front of him, and with a convulsion of his whole being, took off his coat.

" Listenterme, gen'l'men," he implored, now squinting. He pointed to the spotted handkerchief round his face. Then he ripped it off, revealing a huge swelling of the left cheek; and he delivered it a terrific blow with his right fist.

" Tumer!" he screamed. " P'raps a cancer. See? Jerthink I'm 'ere terday because I want ter be 'ere? Listen, gen'l'men; listenterme. My medical adviser warned me that if I sermuch as put me foot out of bed on a day like this, 'e washes 'is 'ands of the case and 'e tole me to take another erpinion."

He smote the swelling even harder than before.

"Christ, gen'l'men; I've got me livin' to make. I can't afford to neglec' me clients. 'Speshally when I've got the goods. See? So, come on, gen'l'men, for the love of Gord. I'm tellin' yer, 'ere it is. In these henvelopes. The nime of the winner of the November 'Andicap for nineteen 'undred and ite. Ten shillin's and it's yours. Christ. Ten shillin's the packet. Goin', goin'—gen'l'men—gone!"

Still nobody moved. He was obliged to spit out a mouthful of disgust at human lack of faith. Like a man whose patience could not reasonably or decently be expected to hold out much longer, he said:

"Very well, gen'l'men. Very well. I'll tell yer wot I'll do. Pay me a shillin'—Christ, a shillin'—for the envelopes, and when you've backed the 'orse and it *walks* 'ome, you can come 'ere, on this sime spot, and you can pay me the difference—nine bob each. There yer are, gen'l'men. That's wot I'll do. I put yer on yer 'onour. A shillin' the packet, and after the race and you've seen the 'orse *walk* 'ome, you'll find me 'ere, always yours truly, on this sime spot. A shillin' each. Jesus!"

One of the crowd, shabby and as hungry as the man himself, stepped forward and bought an envelope. Then the crowd followed suit. In a few moments the stock was gone. I myself invested a shilling. The name of the horse subsequently proved to be that of a non-starter; and when all is said and done no tip could be more satisfactory. It brings relief immediately after the race, and it leaves you fresh to bet another day. When the man had sold out he retied the bandage round his face, put on his coat, and vanished into the mist, followed by the first of his reluctant customers.

The glossy indifference of the horses, the mouths in the corner on the faces of bookmakers, the solitariness of jockeys; the solemnity of the "tic-tac" men, the concealed anxiety of all trainers, the sweep of an English sky over the course, and the pageantry of fashion—and the scum. I suppose it is a great sport; but I quickly found the boring sameness of it all, and of all the crowds that go to race-meetings. The history is there, I admit, the background of time; the Derby in a snowstorm; Lord Rosebery and Lily Langtry, and the Blue Riband of the Turf and Prime Minister of England; the pictures of "Spy" in the clubs. Tattersall's and Tod Sloan and Lord Lansdowne. There is drama, too, and the great roar "They're off," and the knowledge that all the country, town and village, is in suspense. But I cannot keep myself interested in excitement only. No game rises to national greatness if it has not been played some time or other by the crowds who watch. Also it must go back to boyhood; at least that is the way I see any game that draws its genius from the English people.

It is a curious fact that I, the last man in the world to seek interest in sport or to be called an "out-of-door man," wrote cricket reports for a newspaper that, alone of all in the English-speaking world, did not publish racing news, no programme or betting or forecasts. On the occasion of a great race, such as the Grand National or the Derby, the *Manchester Guardian* would send somebody to describe it as part of the English scene; and many columns of literature, vivid and human, picturesque and humorous, have appeared next day from the pens of James Bone, Ivor Brown, A. V. Cookman, Gordon Phillips, George Leach, H. Boardman. Occasionally an article would be printed in the *Guardian* before the race, discussing the horses from an abstract view of breeding and form; but no open show of tipping was permitted. None the less, E. J. Phillips, the writer of the article, often was as wise as any of the avowed racing correspondents in his oblique "fancies." Steve Donoghue once stated that he read none but the racing articles in the "M.G." because no other newspaper "wrote so beautifully about the horses."

The *Guardian's* persistent boycott of the "Turf" as a daily feature in its columns is the most astounding fact in English journalism; it is, indeed, almost incredible, for in no other newspaper is sport so extensively and thoroughly covered, not excluding "soccer" football, in spite of its recent associations with filthy lucre in the shape of vast transfer fees for professionals (one week a man named McTaggart might win a match for Sheffield United and the next week score the goal that defeats Sheffield United), and the "pools" of Mr. Littlewood.

At the dawn of 1921, on New Year's Day in fact, I awoke at five or six in the morning suffering a sensation the like of which I had not known before. It was as though a garden rake were being clumsily and impatiently drawn through my bowels. For a year or two I had known terrific pains in the stomach two or three hours after a meal. I often bent myself hard over a table to ease one sort of ache by provoking another. I consumed vast amounts of charcoal biscuits and bismuth. The cause of the trouble was poor and insufficient food and a nervous system agitated by the fact that C. P. Scott was using me as one of his secretaries.

When the fangs of the garden rake had got into my vitals, I realised that this was a crisis in my affairs. Here was no ordinary agony; its rhythm and tidal wave were spectacular. My bedroom was in a back attic, and my landlady and her husband slept on the floor below, at the front of the house. No telephones or bells, needless to say. My problem was how to get to the bathroom and drink a tumbler of hot water before death claimed me. My main thought was of my wretched luck. Damn me if the fates were not after all going to run me out just as I was getting set: I had only recently found myself on the *Manchester Guardian* after years of bitter hardship and frustration.

The sweat that dropped from my brow was caused as much by indignation as by physical torture. The whole of the will to live in me was concentrated in a determination to reach the bathroom. My belief in hot water in those days amounted to a superstition. At first I had no leisure to feel afraid, though my reason told me that I was more or less *in extremis*. The bathroom, the bathroom! For an eternity I levered myself into a position more or less upright, then a vicious pull of the rake dragged me from the bed to the floor. I was now dimly conscious of a most disturbing sound in the silence of the dawn, a dreadful moan ; it emanated from myself, with effects so blood-curdling that panic overcame me at last, and I fainted. The moan fortunately awakened the landlady. I was put to bed, and a doctor was fetched. He advised an operation on the bowels but I decided to to trust to nature. For three months I remained in bed ; my diet for days was barley water. A tumbler of castor oil (the last resort of a good old-fashioned "G.P.") removed some considerable impediment inside me.

I wallowed in convalescence. On dark February nights I heard the hurry of feet in the streets below and the pelt of rain on the bedroom window. The fire flickered on the ceiling ; the nurse dozed off. It was the first time in my life that I had known the bliss of irresponsibility, of a sensual savouring of my own frail state, of being looked after. I was worn so thin that when I saw myself naked in a mirror I wept. It was a shame.

Then the renewal. I would lie in bed and feel the quiet glow of the return of health. One day I was permitted to sit up and eat cold chicken, with a glass of cold water. Few experiences of mine in the world of æsthetic delights have equalled this relish of carnal appetite. To rise from a sick-bed each morning, while the sheets were smoothed, to get back into haven again, to attain release and safe recumbance after much tottering, with weakness filling my eyes with tears of self-pity—bliss was it then to feel half-alive ! And the sense of a wholesale clearing out, as of a great flush of water in the lavatory of your whole being.

I dwell on this illness because it made me again, as

body and as spirit. A severe illness in the late twenties is symbolical. It is the time when your destiny must change gear if a new direction is to be taken. You are young enough, if you survive, to feel the miracle of resurrection, a beginning again; it is as though you had been subjected to an assize of the gods and granted another lease of fortune. That, at any rate, was my self-satisfied feeling when in the spring of 1921 I saw the buds in the trees, and walked upright upon the earth again, and ate food good to taste, no bismuth afterwards but a half-bottle of Burgundy with dinner every evening; for astonishingly did my doctor insist that I must now depart from a lifetime's abstinence from alcoholic liquor. By the time May came in 1921, and its floods of sunshine that were not dimmed on any day of that summer until August, I was filled by a vibration of well-being and confidence not often known to me before. This was my Anno Mirabilis, and I knew it.

In 1921 I became definitely known as a *Manchester Guardian* writer, not, maybe, dealing with the subjects I had set myself to expound, such as music, metaphysics, all literature, drama, economics, politics and God knows what all. To retain health I was asked by W. P. Crozier to write for the "M.G." on cricket throughout the summer, to go up and down the land day after day. The Australians were in England; this was the season of Armstrong's conquering hosts. So at last the dearest dream of my boyhood came true. I went to Lord's one spring afternoon to watch the Australians at the nets. The time of day was towards half-past five; rain had fallen slightly, but now the sun shone and the grass glittered and the fresh breeze was sweet and the birds sang in the trees at the Nursery end. Years and years before, when I roamed the streets of my native city or played cricket on the brickcrofts and waste lands, I had murmured to myself the wonderful phrase which so many times appeared in the cricket reports of the period: "Richardson relieved Lockwood at the Nursery end"; "Ranjitsinhji glanced Jones to the ropes at the Nursery end." And here I was, at long last, actually present at the Nursery, walking from net to net, watching Australians at practice. And all around me London, London waiting on a summer night.

This year I wrote my first Test Match reports. In June, 1921, I took a first-class railway pass and several five-pound notes from the cashier of the *Manchester Guardian*, and one Friday, just as everybody was returning to office and workshop after lunch, I departed from London Road station to Nottingham. A bedroom had been reserved for me at the Flying Horse, a real hotel, with bars and smoke-rooms and a wine-list. My immediate job on reaching Nottingham was to go to Trent Bridge, look at the wicket, and send a short preliminary article called "Test Match Prospects" to my paper. I took a tram to Trent Bridge, walked across the wide river, saw the famous ground where I had sent my dreams on many a day of hot summer, sent them from the prison of a class-room at school, while lessons were mumbled and I saw, far away, the lovely cover drive of R. H. Spooner, my idol, my hero.

I confess that I did not enter the gates of Trent Bridge and inspect the wicket. I carried a Press pass in my pocket; but my courage failed at the pinch. I glanced through the main gates and saw one or two men with cameras; they looked alarmingly efficient and possessive. So I returned to Nottingham and bought an evening paper and learned that the groundsman at Trent Bridge had expressed the opinion that if no more rain fell the Test Match wicket to-morrow would be a "beauty." Here was material enough for a half a column of decoration—historical Trent Bridge, Arthur Shrewsbury, William Gunn and so on. It was in this, the first of all of my thousands of telegraphed messages to the "M.G.," that I invented the phrase about Trent Bridge being a cricketer's Lotos-land—"where it is always afternoon and 365 for 4." I was very pleased with it. I composed the message standing up at one of the desks in the G.P.O.—always one of my favourite places for writing—and I handed it to a clerk behind the counter and gave him also a telegraph-pass. From a concealed spot, I watched him count the pages and put them aside on a pile of other papers. I was satisfied that my article would never be heard of again, never reach the office of the "M.G." in Manchester. But it did. There, next morning, was the half-column, with (for the "M.G.") the strident heading:

TO-DAY'S TEST MATCH

INTERESTING PROSPECT AT NOTTINGHAM

By "Cricketer"

"Cricketer" was a nom-de-plume enforced on me by W. P. Crozier, who argued that the public seldom remembered initials; and in those days nobody was allowed to sign a name in full in the "M.G." After a week-end of cogitation I could evolve nothing more brilliant than "Long Stop" or "Googlie." He also lacked originality; I think his suggestion was "Old Trafford." His secretary, Madeleine Linford, happened to be present and heard our discussion, and she said, "Why not call yourself 'Cricketer'?" I was, I am afraid, ribald. "'Cricketer'?" I said; "I suppose if it had been football you'd have suggested 'Footballer'?" But Crozier, with his customary quick sense of the fitness of all things for the "M.G.," said, "Excellent!" Thus was "Cricketer" born and baptized.

It was the custom of the period for sporting journalists to use pen-names, especially in the North of England. My Lancashire press-colleagues included three famous veterans. First of all there was J. A. H. Catton, editor of the *Athletic News*, incredibly small in height, red in the face, round as a ball, gold spectacles, white moustache, bald head at the front, twinkling eyes; he was as though born from Bacchus out of Mr. Pickwick. He had spent a wild youth but was now reformed, and when he visited London he stayed at the Thackeray Temperance Hotel. He would describe with great glee, tears of happiness in his eyes, sparkle of perspiration on his forehead, how during an English Cup Final he had slept throughout the game on the floor at the back of the Press Box—"dead drunk." He wrote under the name of "Tityrus," and was one of the first of the poetic school of cricket reporters; he seldom referred to a cricket ball. It was for him " the crimson rambler."

There was Arthur Brierley, representative of a newspaper circulating through the hinterland of Lancashire county, notably Preston, a sterling and honest craftsman. He was a rather fierce-looking man, hinting of a high blood-pressure and he wore a belligerent moustache. He flew into tempers on very slight provocation. He and Jimmy Catton, life-long friends and rivals, occasionally achieved volcanoes and siroccos of enmity in the Press Box. They both observed that conscientious habit of taking a note of every ball bowled in a match, as much as and even more detail than that of the official scorers. Every ball a dot, and what happened to it, how many runs scored from it and by which batsman and in what direction of the field. Never was this wealth of minutæ reflected in the reports written by Jimmy or Arthur. The accountancy was a ritual ; they preserved the statistics in pocket-books, and they could, at notice, produce a documented history of any important match in which England or Lancashire had played covering a period of more than a quarter of a century. Catton once showed me the complete note of A. C. Maclaren's innings of 424, scored at Taunton ; each ball, who bowled it, and how the master dealt with it.

When a batsman got out Jimmy and Arthur would confer. " I make him four hours and thirty-three minutes "—meaning the duration of the innings—" Five fours, nine threes, and sixteen twos, and twenty-five singles." A dreadful disturbance happened without warning on a lazy afternoon at Leicester, in the remote past, before the pretty field was spoiled by lime-kilns.

Two Leicestershire batsmen made a long somnolent stand in the comfortable Midland warmth. There was little to write about, and even Jimmy relaxed to the extent of smoking his pipe, all the time, of course, marking down his dots. At last the partnership was broken. Following a silence denoting much mental arithmetic, Arthur spoke.

" Three hours fifty, Jimmy. Twelve fours, three threes, six twos." A pause. Then Jimmy replied: " No, Arthur. Eleven fours, I think." " *Twelve*, Jimmy." They went through them one by one. " He began with four to leg off Cook. Then after a single which took him opposite Tyldesley, there was one past cover." And so on. The crisis occurred when Arthur asseverated:

" No, Jimmy. That was at the other end. He scored a single from the sixth ball. You've credited Coe with a four belonging to him."

" Arthur; you're wrong. I'm not in the habit of making mistakes of that kind. You're taking on too much agency work. I've told you before. You can't send four messages every half-hour and get the figures down right. Eleven fours; Arthur. And don't lose your temper, if you can help it."

Arthur had abruptly gone very purple. " Don't you damn well tell me not to lose my temper, Jimmy. I've been at this job as long as you, or as near as makes no damn difference. Don't be so damned patronising, if you *don't* mind. As for too much work, why if it damn well comes to that . . ." In a few minutes both of them were on their feet and Arthur's moustache was gnawing itself within a few inches of Jimmy's. Then they would remember the dignity of the Press. The storm would rumble away; but for hours afterwards a newcomer to the box might well have thought they were strangers, polite but not acquainted.

The third of my veteran colleagues of the North was John Clegg; he represented the *Manchester Evening News*, and made no pretence either to literature or statistics. He waited until Jimmy or Arthur had announced the balance-sheet, and carried it unanimously, so to say. His style related him to a classic period of sporting journalism: "Lancashire, having won the toss, elected to bat. "Brearley went on at the Manchester end, vice Dean." "With his score at 37, Fry apparently offered a palpable chance to the slips, which was not taken." "After a brief stoppage owing to rain, the match was resumed at 3.30. Handicapped by the slippery ball, Hirst had recourse to the sawdust." Clegg made no pretensions at all; he kept no notes and, whatever the state of the game, he "had recourse" to the refreshment bar at fixed intervals. He left the match as soon as his duties, exclusively performed for an evening paper, finished at half-past four. He openly rejoiced whenever it rained. Once I arrived late at Old Trafford, after a journey from Lord's. It was the lunch interval, and the scoreboard announced that Lancashire against Northamptonshire had lost five wickets for fifty on a dull morning threatening bad weather. I met Clegg as soon as I had entered the ground and realised the dismal situation of the Lancashire side. "Looks very bad," I said to Clegg; but after an inspection of the clouds above, he said, "Too high, I'm afraid, too high."

Each of these great old characters wrote about football in winter. Clegg, again with no nonsense about him, used only his initials. He was the happiest of men, and very courtly. He was usually late in arriving at the Press Box, and always the first to leave. He wore a curved moustache and seemed by habit always to be wiping moisture from it with the back of his right hand. In the football season the prose style of all three observed the unities. A goalkeeper was " the custodian " ; the goal was " the citadel." Wherever the match happened to be taking place was the " venue." Arthur, by the way, signed himself " Perseus," winter and summer. Clegg disliked Arthur's austerity ; at lunch-time Arthur usually remained in the Press Box and ate out of an attaché-case hidden under the writing-desk. One day, a moment or two before the luncheon interval, Arthur was called to the telephone outside the box. While he was absent, Clegg crept on tiptoe to Brierley's seat, opened the attaché-case, and exhibited its contents on high, water-cress or tomato sandwiches and a piece of currant cake. " Gentlemen," said Clegg, " observe—Arthur's Bacchanalian Feast ! " This was Clegg's one and only deliberate attempt at irony.

It says much for the tolerance of these magnificent old stagers that they received me hospitably into the Press Box for all my purple periods and classical allusions. I tremble to-day to imagine what they really thought of my preliminary lucubrations—Macartney, the Figaro of cricket ; J. W. Hearne, the Turveydrop of the crease, not to mention Maclaren as Don Quixote, and his stonewalling partner, Makepeace, the Sancho Panza ! To say the truth and to pay justice to their comradeship, I found after a while that all the time they had liked, and even, in a way, had admired my writings.

But not all at once did I dare go into the company of the elect, especially when I visited Lord's. I was diffident about the aristocratic Sydney Pardon, editor of *Wisden*; he would glance at me with his quizzical, experienced eyes, and I decided he was putting me down mentally as an enthusiastic provincial. He was distinguished and mellow, a little sandy and not tall; but his moustache told you of London and Lord's and Covent Garden. The warts on his face only emphasised his experience. The lids would fall over his eyes and, once again, nature lent an air of subtlety to one whom subsequently I came to know as a typical English gentleman of the middle classes and a fanatical lover of Wagner. He was a connoisseur of the turf, and none but the classic races interested him; he would put his money only on thoroughbreds. He was terribly short-sighted and watched every ball at cricket through opera-glasses; rightly he would not wear spectacles, but a pince-nez with a cord would have become him. To talk to him about the game was like talking to George Saintsbury about wines.

There was Stuart Caine, too, who succeeded Pardon as editor of *Wisden*, the most embracingly courteous man I have ever known, big and stout and capacious, who would bow to you and give you precedence even at the entrance to a gentleman's lavatory. Now and again, Bettesworth of the *Field* would come into the Press Box, collecting paragraphs for his unique weekly column, which would tell you how this bowler measured his run, and how he twiddled his little finger; or how that batsman shuffled his feet three times before settling down. Bettesworth was subject to attacks of sensational deafness, and for days he would be cut off from the outer world; but this was no handicap to conversations which he liked to hold with himself. One hot day at Lord's a long stand was imperceptibly proceeding through the sweltering hours; the bowlers seemed helpless, and the experts in the Press Box began to talk about the malign effect on modern cricket of the groundsman and his ten-ton roller.

"It's killing the game!" "Not fair to the bowlers!" "The wicket is doped!" And so on. Suddenly, during a momentary silence, old Bettesworth was heard to say to himself with quite an impatient forcibility, "Can't understand it! Nobody seems to be spinning the ball! That pitch is full of spots. J. T. Hearne would have been simply unplayable from the pavilion end. Poor wickets at Lord's nowadays!"

H. J. Henley, with his Johnsonian stick and his ability to stand at the bar at the Oval for an hour on end and yet not miss any bit of play that crucially influenced the match; "Bill" Pollock, with his black hat and preoccupied air, until he had found his daily "wisecrack" for the *Express*—"Nothing succeeds like Sussex"—then he would drop years from his face and shoulders and go at once for a pint of cold beer. In later years, the box has been enriched by Robertson-Glasgow, a fine bowler when he played for Oxford University, Somersetshire, and the Gentlemen; tall and handsome and agile, dome of forehead and as charged with brain and wit as anybody. I stood with him one afternoon at Lord's at the bar under the grandstand, where the alley-way leads to the practice ground. All sorts and conditions of members of the M.C.C. go to the practice nets at Lord's towards the fall of the day, and this time a genuine relic went past, armed with pads and carrying a venerable bat; he was himself very old, and bent at the knees, with grizzled white moustache and a nose of considerable cellarage. On his head was a yellow-striped cap reminiscent of W. G. Grace. As he tottered feebly but determinedly towards the nets, Robertson-Glasgow viewed him admiringly, then said to me, " When *he's* out, you know, we're all out! "

I have loved every minute of the many days I have lived at Lord's, and not only when I have actually been there but when I have journeyed to it on summer mornings. The ritual began from the moment I came out of my club and called a taxi and said " Lord's! " The taxi-man felt some pleasure in it too: " Lord's, yessir! "

With the leisure that only a London taxi-man retains amongst drivers of vehicles in this age of pace, propulsion and explosion, we would proceed along the Haymarket, across Piccadilly, and soon we would be in Baker Street, which was still freshly aired, with the shops pleasantly occupied and old ladies out with their dogs, and one or two tight-trousered old gentlemen doddering along. Baker Street, where Sherlock Holmes had lived! I had read about it in the *Strand Magazine* in the free libraries of my remote youth; and here I was on the way to Lord's in a taxi. Also I had read, when I was a boy, about the West End clubman, and I had imagined him as of rich purple visage, sitting in the windows of Pall Mall, with nothing to do all day but function as West End clubman. And here, mirabile dictu! was I myself a West End clubman. I never seriously believed that I looked the part.

Along Regent's Park the taxi ambled and the boats were sailing on the lake and the children played with the ducks and offered them pieces of bread by tentative holdings out of their tiny hands, and the spring day and the spirit of London blessed the scene.

The taxi drew up at last outside the W. G. Grace gates; inside we could catch a glimpse of the crocuses, brought up to sport the M.C.C. colours. Now the vision of the pavilion and the field and the high white stand near the Nursery where the trees beyond barely rippled. Then the first sojourn, sitting on the Green Bank; you could see the cricket in snatches from under the awning over the seats in front. I have sat on the Green Bank at Lord's through a lifetime of June afternoons, when the play has not protested too much, but has moved to the evening's slanting light, as gentle as muted strings accompanying the summer's passing show at Lord's; all the life of the town in promenade; not a menacing cloud in the heavens.

But Lord's was not all patrician and school tie. It was (and is, God willing) a microcosm of London itself. For Lord's had its East End as well as its West End. The pavilion and the terrace near the Green Bank were not more a part of the pageant of Lord's than the humour and elbow-to-elbow traffic outside the Tavern. Here was the "crowd," a motley of Camberwell and Putney and St. John's Wood and Balham; artisans, actors—some of them visibly "resting"; butchers, bakers, candlestick-makers; Chelsea veterans vibrant with medals; Cockneys and comedians and keepers of stage-doors; scribes from Fleet Street and trombone-players from Queen's Hall. Now and again one of the nobility, direct from the pavilion, might come to the Tavern and drink a tankard, talking with the next man at the counter and watching the game out of the corner of his failing eye. Hearts just as proud and fair may beat in Belgrave Square.

There are all sorts of nooks and crannies and "back-stage" activities at Lord's. I have seen gilded ducal chairs being carried out of the pavilion's doors at the rear ("tradesman's entrance"). The printing shop under the grandstand is busy all day with the "fall of the last wicket." Hens used to pick their way about the practice ground and once I saw a hen go into a gentlemen's lavatory at Lord's. A notice in severe type, rather in the nature of a Proclamation, warns small boys that if they ask the players for autographs they will be "removed" from the premises; but no small boy at Lord's has ever been known to suffer removal.

Lord's is representative of London in a way beyond the understanding of the foreign visitor, representative of that nice social balance held by the English, whereby privilege and prerogative may hob-nob with the servants downstairs and not feel too sure of themselves either.

As the afternoon comes to an end, the pavilion is

draped in a great velvet shadow; the sun shines now on the high stand opposite the far Nursery end. The pigeons walk under the feet of deep long-off; the Tavern empties and goes reluctantly home. The bell of the clock in the tower covered with ivy chimes half-past six, and the cricketers come from the field in groups of twos and threes, and last of all, the umpires follow with the stumps gathered in their arms. I have lingered on at Lord's, sitting until I have been alone on the high stand under the trees, so close to the clock that I could hear it ticking. Then out into the St. John's Wood Road again, and now another taxi back to London, the private cars already flashing from their interiors the white of immaculate shirt and the rich brocade of evening gown; while the buses go down Regent Street towards Piccadilly Circus, red in the first fires of the sunset.

Unless the occasion were a Test Match with the ground congested, I seldom sat in the Press Box until it was time for me, after the tea interval, to write my daily fifteen hundred words. I preferred to stay in the fresh air, walking on the grass at country places such as Tonbridge, Canterbury, Cheltenham, Gloucester, Worcester and Dover. The hours I have stood behind the screen at the bowler's end!—or wandered round the little crowd as it sat on wooden benches, quiet and companionable, while the day passed from noon to evening, a glass of beer and a sandwich for lunch in a tent. At Trent Bridge I would loll on top of the pavilion, the cricketers below, or, if play were boring, I would mingle with the opulent cars lining one side of the field, the gentry of Nottinghamshire watching from the leathered stuffy interiors, rugs and thermos flasks and old red-faced men or imposing dowagers, or pretty girls. Or I would lose sight of the match altogether by going behind the pavilion—it is always somehow fascinating to turn one's back on a match for a period, to know that it is still happening while you are not looking at it.

One day I was coming from cricket in Southampton. The match had finished at noon on the third morning, and as I took a short-cut back to town I lost my bearings. I found myself walking along a cindered pathway with the brick walls of private gardens on one side, and on the other a stretch of allotments. Not a living soul was present except myself; not a material sound was to be heard save the crunching of my footsteps. I could hear the summer running away. I experienced a heightened sense of isolation in or from space; only time was real, time as shimmering daylight. Suddenly a girl came through one of the doors of the private gardens. She wore a white open-necked blouse and a blue skirt, and her hair was fair and surrounded by sunshine. A glossy young black spaniel ran in front of her, nosing the ground in an ecstasy of freedom; he leapt up at me and with the indiscriminate friendliness of his kind, he licked my hand, leaving it wet and cool. I patted his head of silk, and the girl and myself exchanged smiles; then she passed by me on her way, and disappeared round a bend of the path, the dog scampering in a panic after her; he had seemed for a while to consider transferring his allegiance and remaining with me for the rest of his life. This moment of segregated time, and this simple everyday occurrence has never faded from my memory; it was all symbolical in a way I cannot and do not wish to analyse. I, too, went on my way and in a few minutes arrived at the main road leading into Southampton, again part of the perpetual current and traffic of general existence.

Soon I reached the inn where we were all staying. In the bar the Lancashire cricketers had already come back from the match. There was Harry Dean, a hero of my boyhood, now entering on his last years in the field. I had seen him through many summers bowling for Lancashire in the pomp of Maclaren's day, a willing horse and a Lancashire lad from the richest soil. He wore blue serge and a watch-chain across his waistcoat, and strong boots. The old professional cricketers did not go to the cinema theatres in the evenings after a long day's play; they sat in bar-parlours and talked cricket. Or you would see them walking slowly and gravely along the streets, two by two, hands in pockets, and smoking their pipes. There was also "Lol" Cook, bosom friend of Dean, and he was a portly little man whose head hung on one side in a sort of patient acquiescence to a world that was always expecting him to bowl against the wind and would so seldom see eye to eye with him in appeals for leg before wicket. Harry Dean spoke with a deliberate accent, the purest Lancashire, and by his use of certain words and cadences revealed that he had once on a time attended Sunday School and had escaped the advancing blight of industrialism and half-education. He would utter audible capital letters when he extolled the great cricketers of the time of his apprenticeship. " The reason why we young 'uns learned t' Principles was that we pla-ayed with Wise Men. It were an Education to bat wi' Maister Spooner "—(Harry, by the way, was usually number ten in the order of the innings, and his one and only stroke was an elegant but unproductive forward push, usually straight back to the bowler)—" aye, it were an Education. And Maister Maclaren were a Great Captain, and once at Kennington Oval he coom in dressing-room before, start of match and said, 'Harry, I've lost toss, so put on three pairs of socks. You'll open at Pavilion end and you'll be bowlin' at half-past six, if I'm not mistaken, because that bloody villain, Sam Apted, has made one of his Shirt Front Wickets.' And, by gum, Maister Maclaren were reight ; Ah were. Ah bowled mi left toe-nail raw that day and Tom Hayward made two 'undred fit for Buckingham Palace. Hey, bah gum, and that was day when Jimmy 'Eap come back in team after 'e'd been dropped. . . ."

James Heap was a slow left-hand spinner with a charming action, a little jump, right hand pointing to heaven, side to the batsman, then a " swing-through " of easeful rhythm. On a " sticky " wicket he could bowl as dangerously as Rhodes himself ; but his misfortune was lumbago. For weeks in dry weather, and on cruel hard wickets, he would slave away spinless and harmless. Then the weather would break ; he would hear the rain in the night and chuckle. But alas ! to quote his own account of the tragedy—" in t' mornin', Maister Maclaren coom into t' dressin'-room, and says,

'At last, Jimmy, you've got your "sticky" wicket! I'll put you on right away—and it's a real "glue-pot" already, and made for you, my lad!'" But, continued Heap, "Ah as to tell im 'Ah'm sorry, Maister Maclaren, but Ah can 'ardly stand oop this mornin'—lumbago's coom back.'"

But Harry Dean must be allowed to continue his own story of Jimmy: "Aye it were same day Jimmy 'Eap were back in team. Maister Maclaren 'ad dropped 'im because on t' 'ard wickets 'e couldn't spin 'em, and when they were 'sticky' 'e were a martyr to t' lumbago. So Jimmy meks oop 'is mind to earn 'is pla-ace in team wi' 'is battin' and fieldin'; and 'e does so well wi' second eleven that 'e's invited to join us on t' Southern tour. And so there 'e was, fieldin' mid-off at t' Oval, 'ot as Ah've ever known it, and before we begins, and Ah'm gettin' ready to bowl, Jimmy coom to me and says, 'Ah'll show 'em; Ah feels fit as a two-year-old to-day, 'Arry.' And, bah gum, no sooner 'ad match started when Tom Haywood drives one right past Jimmy to t' far Vauxhall end, and Jimmy set off after it, elbers up like a 'undred-yards championship. 'E picks ball oop reight on t' edge of boundary, and throws it back—all in one action, with plenty of 'fluence, then cooms runnin' back to 'is place at mid-off, not far from me; and 'e says, a little bit out 'o breath, 'Just stopped 'er as she was goin' for four, 'Arry.' 'Aye, Jimmy,' so Ah 'ad to tell 'im, 'They run five.' And then, just as slips were gettin' ready to bend down for t' next ball, and Maister Maclaren were plucking up 'is trousers, 'e just calls out to Maister Spooner, 'I say, Reggie, have you ever seen those old spavined cab-horses outside Paddington Station ? ' That's all 'e said, and bah gum, Ah laughed so much that me next ball were full-toss, and Tom 'Ayward put it over t' ropes and Maister Maclaren shouted, ' Hey, 'Eap, you needn't go after that one ! ' Aye, it were a pleasure to pla-ay with Maister Maclaren, and Maister Spooner, and such men." I asked him if he hadn't sometimes felt the futility of bowling at Ranjitsinhji on a perfect wicket. " Noa," he replied, temperately ; " noa ; it were a tough proposition, and no mistake ; but Ah never give up hope. Ah used to say to meself, ' Well, 'Arry, it's his brain against thine ! "

In recent years professional cricketers have achieved much in the way of liberty, equality and fraternity ; they do not call the captain " sir " when they speak to him ; their greeting is a familiar " Good mornin', Skipper " and they are as well-dressed as he, probably suede shoes, never the hob-nailed hardware of Harry Dean. But none of these modern products of the new order can attain the dignity which descended on the " old pro." when he touched his forehead to " Maister Maclaren." The most lordly of cricketers—this same Maclaren—once told me how, on coming from the field after making a majestic century, he was met on his way to the " Amateurs' " dressing-room by Harry Dean, who with his finger to his forehead, said, " Well pla-ayed, sir, it were grand." Maclaren added that this was a compliment worth having, from a man who himself was a master of his craft, a bowler who whenever he sent down a loose ball on the leg side, after having agreed to Maclaren's mainly offside field, would immediately apologise, " Sorry, sir—she slipped."

The county cricketer has become in certain instances a man of a bourgeois profession; he has his pride as well as his suede shoes. One morning not many years ago a professional cricketer, a slow left-arm spin bowler, approached his captain shortly before the beginning of a match and announced he wouldn't be able to play. " But why, Joe; what's wrong?" asked the perturbed captain. " Me finger," said Joe, " just bust it, Skipper." There was then a careful examination of the wound; I was also permitted to take a look, and I detected at length a slight discoloration of the nail of the forefinger of the left hand. " But, Joe," I could not resist saying, " you're supposed to be a slow spin bowler—not Kreisler."

VII

I WAS well in my teens before I went to concerts or knew much of music, but I cannot remember when I was not interested and excited about the theatre. This fact is, to use the phrase of Carlyle, significant of much. Forty-five years ago music was for the few and not the many; it was almost the prerogative of the middle and upper classes. To go to a theatre was as natural a perquisite of the poor and the half-educated as oranges and football matches.

Forty years ago the theatre had not yet been rendered culture-conscious. The influence of Ibsen and Shaw remained more or less confined to stage societies and independent theatres and other esoteric organisations in London. The theatre was still generally known as "the stage," an embracing term which covered any activity behind the footlights from *Hamlet* to *Charley's Aunt* (with W. S. Penley). There was—perhaps still is—a weekly paper called *The Stage*, the front page full of advertisements: "Henry St. Clair: 27 Maida Vale: Resting"; and columns of the companies on tour—*The Sign of the Cross*, B. Company, Wolverhampton T.R., and so on. The actor-managers who ruled over us were descended, no matter how cunningly the family tree divagated, from Mr. Vincent Crummles. They believed that the drama's laws the drama's patrons give; and in one and the same week during an "autumn season" in the provinces, it was possible to see Martin Harvey in *The Only Way* one night, and in Maeterlinck the next. Beerbohm Tree would act melodrama at a matinée—*The Red Lamp* or his masterpiece of sumptuous exotic villainy Isador Izard in *Business is Business*; and on the evening of the same day he would appear fantastically apparelled as Malvolio. The theatre had not yet lost the sniff and smell of naphtha; the genealogy was vivid and unmistakable. The actor-managers wore astrakhan on their overcoat collars, and were shaven purple. They were redolent of the footlights. It was possible to pick them out from the crowds in the city streets; you could see them "crossing stage to right." They were our gods and heroes, they walked as men apart, not of the common air or element. When Henry Irving arrived in Manchester for a fortnight's season at the Theatre Royal, everybody knew he was there, staying at the Queen's Hotel. No "publicity" or interviews announced his coming; such proclamations would have been superfluous. It was a case of a planet ascendant; we did not call them "stars" for nothing. Sometimes I would try to think of Irving doing ordinary things, taking off his trousers before getting into bed, putting his money on the dressing-table, and other acts common to normal beings, but my imagination failed. When his sudden death was announced early on an October morning in 1905, I was walking down Bridge Street, Manchester, going to my job as an office-boy;

the newsboys came tearing down the pavements screaming "Speshul! Death of 'Enry Irving!" The traffic seemed to know of it immediately; there was a perceptible pause in the rumbling of wheels and in the clatter and clop-clop of the hoofs of the great horses that pulled the lorries loaded with bales of merchandise bound for the docks and the Far East. "Death of 'Enry Irving! Speshul!" It was a moment as fraught with national concern as on the night of a few years earlier when the news of the passing of Queen Victoria had come sounding through the fog like a bell, emptying theatres and the city. The death of Henry Irving likewise made a gap in nature.

I cannot pretend that my memory holds accurate impressions of Irving's acting; I was only fifteen years old when he died at Bradford a few hours after he had fallen on his knees in Tennyson's *Becket*, saying:

> *At the right hand of Power,*
> *Power and great glory—for Thy Church, O Lord—*
> *Into Thy hands, O Lord—into Thy hands.*

But, like every other civilised man of my time of life, I wish to die in the belief that I saw him in *The Bells* dusting the snow from his boots, giving to the maidservant an unforgettably gracious smile as he declined her help and took off his own gaiters. The *charm* of these old artists! It was this aristocratic quality of manners and presence that renders superfluous the "new" intellectual criticism's denigrations of their work as a whole. "Ham," they call it, poor things.

How could it matter if Irving would unashamedly play in *Waterloo*, or Forbes Robertson in *Mice and Men*, or Martin Harvey in *The Breed of the Treshams*, or the Terrys in *Sweet Nell of Old Drury*, or John Hare in *A Pair of Spectacles*?; how could it matter that they sponsored rubbish?—for the moment they came on to the stage and let their voices be heard, an aroma of charm and ripe companionable embracement of the audience and the entire theatre worked a spell that defied power of resistance.

As I entered the twenties and became a constant reader of the *Manchester Guardian*, and every Tuesday devoured the paper's two or three long columns of dramatic criticism of Monday night's productions, signed "C.E.M.," "J.E.A.," and "A.N.M.," I imperceptibly adopted the attitude of the newly-arrived intellectual and affected to sniff at the commercial theatre and the actor-manager and Pinero, Sutro and Henry Arthur Jones. The Repertory Movement had reached Manchester, with Miss Horniman the high priestess at the Gaiety Theatre, the same "comedy" theatre in which I had sold chocolates as a boy when it was owned by J. Pitt Hardacre, who was wont to appear without warning in *East Lynne*; he was a sort of Charles Wyndham run to seed, and at last his theatre was temporarily closed by the Manchester Watch Committee as a house of dubious fame. I attended, in the pit, the farewell and "benefit" performance for Hardacre, with a galaxy of names lending sentimental support. Hardacre appeared as Hamlet in the gravediggers' scene, and was rather drunk. I suppose my memory here is not trustworthy; it retains an impression of Hardacre (in black tie and dinner-jacket) taking the words out of the Queen's mouth and jumping into the grave shouting "Shweetsh to the shweetsh!"

The *Manchester Guardian* looked down its nose at Tree, and Arthur Bourchier, and Waller. I fancy it even patronised Seymour Hicks, and sent a young reporter to *The New Clown*, in which James Welch was one of the greatest of comic actors, quiet and melancholy and never for a moment anything but earnest and serious. The higher criticism scared me away from the latest West End successes, though I confess that without a word to my friends I would go, almost disguised, on Friday nights, to catch an atavistic glimpse of Tree as Colonel Newcome singing "Wapping Old Stairs" in a voice palpably quavering, to indicate extreme age and feebleness. At the crack of the *Guardian's* whip we were herded into a dingy Assembly Hall one night to see the first production in Manchester of Ibsen's *Ghosts*; the law prohibited the presentation of this play in any theatre proper, taking money at the box-office, so we pretended to form an Ibsen Society just for one night. Harold Neilson was the pioneer in these provincial austerities. In later years I came to know him as a member of the Middlesex Cricket Club and Lord's, and I have sat for hours with him watching the game on the top of the pavilion, and would never have guessed he was acquainted with Ibsen and had chilled my bone's marrow with thc awful cry, at one and the same time petulant, ghastly, and somehow telling of helpless childish idiocy: "The sun! The sun!"

James Agate, in one of his "Ego" volumes, gives a list of "calls" or "cries" heard on the stage and remembered over a stretch of twenty years—Janet Achurch as Nora and the sudden drop in her voice in her "Let me pass, please," to Dr. Rank; Forbes Robertson's exquisite "Give me that man That is not passion's slave"; Mrs. Pat as Paula Tanqueray saying to her neighbour Mrs. Cortelyon, "I fancy I *have* observed a roof"; Irene Vanbrugh's terrific "I go to no park to-morrow!" in *His House in Order*; Edith Evans's scandalised "A *Hand-bag*!" in *The Importance of being Earnest*. I would add that blood-freezing wail, "The sun! The sun!" of H. V. Neilson; and the snarl of Norman McKinnel as Anthony in *Strife*—"*Cant!*" And, of course, the most famous of all theatre utterances, Mrs. Pat's "Not bloody likely," which not only let the whole cat of the Eliza Doolittle's breeding out of the bag, but for just a flash of an affrightening second suggested that something much worse than "bloody" was about to petrify us. Nobody has said it since as Mrs. Pat said it. Also there was Benson's astounding treatment of "Words, words, words," as Hamlet; he suddenly turned or flipped over the pages of the book in swift contumacious profusion and repeated with buzzing sibilants, "Wordswordswordswordswords-wordswords," in one impatient breath. And Arthur Sinclair's "The whole world is in a terrible state of chassis," in *Juno and the Paycock*. This was the most ripe and recklessly uninhibited and revelatory piece of comedy-acting I have seen in my life. And also his casual, "Phwat—phwat would be the price of consols this mornin' ? " But there is no end to this game, as indeed there is no end to any of Agate's entrancing symposia. All the same, I must not omit Charles Hawtrey's " Blast ye, *scum* ! "

As I tell of my first experiences in the theatre I am not certain that I am not sometimes seeing and feeling them all through the eyes and minds of Montague or Agate or Monkhouse. I read every word they wrote and I did not, of course, go to every performance that inspired them to their pillared columns of prose. If I did not ever really see Coquelin does it greatly matter, since knowing by heart Montague's description of him, I can see Coquelin *sub specie aeternitatis* ?—not having in time and space been seen by me he is seen by me for ever—his Mascarille, " lolling back among the sofa cushions, seemed sometimes scarcely to speak at all ; relish, mischief, triumph in the mere notion of what he was doing emanated from him more directly than through speech ; his eyes beamed till you might think there was some physical emission from them of lucent shafts of high spirits ; his laughing voice simmered and bubbled over as if from some huge inner reservoir of audible enjoyment. . . ."

But neither Montague nor anybody else has written more vividly of an actor, finding the right illumination of words, the graphic images, than Agate of F. R. Benson (whom I not only actually saw in the theatre many times but once bowled out middle-stump on the cricket field for thirty-five stylish runs) : " I can both see and hear Benson come clanking on to the bare stage as Henry V, carrying a mace with a spike-studded ball swinging from it, and saying, 'What's he that wishes so?' as though the fierce young King was in a real paddy with Westmoreland. He had four things most moderns lack—presence, a profile befitting a Roman coin, voice, and virility to make you believe that Orlando overthrew more than his enemies. His vocal effects were astonishing; 'There roared the sea, the trumpet-clangour sounds' understates some of them."

"Come clanking on" is an inspiration—and I fancy it came from "brother Gustav"—for Benson always suggested angularity or a piston-rod sort of gait and propulsion. He possessed power for grotesque shape; he could mingle dignity and *diablerie* in proportion. His Richard III was a masterpiece of crooked, gargoyled irony, of inherited evil, evil attained by royal and satanic prerogative, with humour and relish added. He looked like a mixture of Doré's Dante and Doré's Don Quixote. The critics of the present time have voted almost unanimously that Benson was not a great actor. Genius burned in him in fits and flickers and gusts and garish fires. Besides, whether on the stage or off it, he was a man ravaged by his particular dæmon. Here is the chief difference between the actors of the present and the past; nowadays the dæmon has been got under rational not to say "refeened" control. No contemporary actor is likely to descend to the bathos of Forbes Robertson's Stranger in Jerome K. Jerome's *The Passing of the Third Floor Back*; or to the noisy horseplay of Benson's Petruchio, jumping over tables and baiting Katharina like a bear in a circus; or to the smothered witless immobility of Tree's Falstaff, whose make-up in the part seemed to exhaust all the resources of a pantomime comedian's wardrobe, so structural was his encasement of padded and basketed corpulence that he was rendered entirely out of touch with the external universe; or to the ponderous beetle-browed bull-necked Macbeth of Bourchier, of which Alan Monkhouse said, "Even murder can't be as serious as all that."

It is as easy to avoid the descents, the sublime puerilities of genius (if you have it not) as it is to remain untouched by its transfiguring grace. The actor-manager, as we have noted, cast a wide net; one evening Fred Terry and Julia Neilson swashbuckled and flounced in *Sweet Nell of Old Drury*, and next evening they flashed and sparkled in the swift rapier counterpoint of Benedict and Beatrice; and there has been none to equal them since in it.

Of Forbes Robertson's Hamlet, I am apparently in a minority of one; probably I was too young and twenty-one to appreciate its classical contours. His Hamlet was a scholar with philosophy making for a sort of donnish urbanity. There was little of the poet, nothing for me of temperamental half-lights or hints of unreason and deep-moving ill-directed impulses. He was even affable, and talked to the players like a University Extension lecturer. The most moving Hamlet I have seen is Gielgud's; for he was in tragic thrall from the moment we saw him in scene II, a man apart, sabled of reverie, yet with a poet's resilience at any prompting of wit. He related Hamlet to a modern psychological awareness, but—and this is the point I wish especially to stress—

without denying himself the traditional histrionic opportunities of the part.

But the contemporary actor, taking him as a whole, is simply *not* histrionic; rather I should call him conversational. He is, of course, the natural consequence of the "play of ideas," which occurred as a welcome reaction to the atrophying romantic artificialities of the actor-managers. It is not easy to convey to the theatregoer of to-day the revelation vouchsafed to some of us when we were very young, by the dramatist who transformed the stage into a room, a credible interior, with one wall taken down. My first "realistic" play (the naïveté of our definitions!) was Charles McEvoy's *David Ballard*, a "slice of life," and lo! and behold, it was my own life as I was then enduring it, imprisoned like David Ballard in an office of perpetual Monday mornings. The acting was on the scale of everyday domestic things, and for a while it was engrossing. But the Repertory movement overdid the manner of the gloomily photographic; and not less harmful to acting as art, which implies imaginative powers of evocation, were the plays of Shaw, which now swept into our provincial ken like a constellation of comets.

We were flattered to think that we were in the know; we mentally referred to ourselves whenever the new word "Shavian" was pronounced. But, as I say, the old Adam, the hankering after true histrionics, led us (at any rate I speak for myself) surreptitiously back to the virtuosi and their variations on theatrical themes.

Not until Shaw himself chose a virtuoso and romantic theme for a play did he give a chance for great acting.

The effect in the long run of the "rationalising" of the English theatre was to modify for me one of the raptures of living; for I prefer to sit at home to enjoy the cut and thrust of ideas. If a play does not urgently call for acting I prefer to read it, just as I prefer to study the scores of contemporary composers who do not give the orchestra full scope.

Ibsen was different; he created characters, and Hedda Gabler did not pale into an abstraction of the Loveless Woman even after we had seen Paula Tanqueray the week before—yes, I say this in calculated black and white. For all Pinero's evasions and conventional moral observation, so annoying to Shaw, Pinero was blessed by the only gift that matters in the long-run to a dramatist. The theatre was his element and he sniffed the atmosphere of the stage by right of nature, and wrote plays in which actors and actresses could find scope for protean powers of illusion. Pinero might easily have avoided the psychological evasions which offended Shaw, yet have fallen flat as a dramatist. Shaw himself has steered clear of obvious expressions on the stage of what he accused Pinero of having—"personal amiabilities and beliefs and conventions." But as soon as Shaw's own once unconventional beliefs have gone the way of all purely intellectual conceptions, and have become as conventional as Pinero's, will it be found that he has provided the stuff for actors and actresses of to-morrow and the day after to seize and feed upon? The only plays of Shaw that have not lost their appeal for me are just those which embrace the theatre's own necessary traditions of farce or melodrama or romantic rhetoric—

The Doctor's Dilemma, for example, or *Arms and the Man*, or *The Devil's Disciple*. Wild horses would not drag me again to *Man and Superman*, or to *Candida*. *Saint Joan* is great not only and not mainly because of the mind Shaw brings to the theme, but because the character of Joan and her drama, not to say melodrama, play on our emotions and imagination all the time, even before Shaw gets brilliantly to work. The trouble with Shaw as a playwright is that he has no consistent dramatic power and range ; his people are largely argumentative, lacking grace and subtlety of temperamental transition.

I fear that all this is a terrible apostasy. I have revelled in Shaw so much, and like everybody who was young when I was young, I owe to him more than I can estimate for enlargement of the means to live fully by a sort of spiritual fertilising or quickening of the mind. I have no time for folk who discuss Shaw as intellect without imagination. As a critic he has opened great windows and revealed thrilling vistas. But I am here discussing him as an influence in the theatre, especially as an influence on acting. To act well in a Shaw play needs mainly a tongue as quick and as truly in tune as the fiddle of Heifetz—and a good memory. The rest could be done sitting down—ten Shaws or so, all talking at once.

" To cross the stage to the right " was not a crude convention of acting when Forbes Robertson walked in front of us. " That you will see Forbes Robertson walk across the stage is a sufficient reason for going to a theatre." Thus spake Montague. The contemporary young man, finding himself alone for a moment on the stage in a room, takes out his silver case, opens it, closes it with a snap, and taps his cigarette on it—as dead for the moment and dramatically null and void as the furniture. George Alexander, left alone a while in a Pinero play strode to the shelves; thickly and opulently lined with books, mostly "dummies," but there were one or two real ones, standing straight or realistically aslant. Alexander selected a volume and began to turn the pages with an engrossment so unself-conscious and convincing that I longed to know the title and the author. And when he was interrupted by the entrance of the character for whom he was waiting, you could see him cut off a momentary but growing interest in the book; and he put it back on its shelf carefully in the place where he had found it. There is no conventional "old-fashionedness" whenever the imagination creates the essential and inner time and place.

The insistence on literalness, on obvious semblances to the present (but passing) show of things and ideas is, at bottom, prosaic. The greatest play of our time, *Juno and the Paycock*, is, for all its "realism," its ruthless and Gargantuan spewing-out of Irish fecklessness, at bottom mingled farce and melodrama. The humour of Captain Doyle and the Joxer is raised to the poetic, by a gusto of imagination not responsible to moral or social conscience. Such a play is neither "fair" nor "unfair" to the Irish; it elevates laughter, tragedy, love, meanness, devotion and indifference to the plane of the heroic. The collapse of Doyle at the end, the thud of the back of his drunken head to the bare boards of the sold-up tenement room, visible symbol of ruin and hopeless, shiftless travail, is even a triumphant announcement. "The who-ole worl' is in a mo-ost ter'rble stashe of chassis!" The play will be none the less true or less violently and richly polyphonic in its gales of nature ripe and rotten, even if the whole world, and Ireland herself, should one day enter and join as one family in an earthly paradise. It is necessary for a newspaper to be up to date, not a play, or even a theatre. "Where *I* happen to act," said Bernhardt when somebody once complained at her "bad taste" for appearing in a play in Wanamakers Store in New York, "where *I* happen to act, is a *theatre*!" And with all their intellectual limitations, wherever the actor-managers chanced to appear, was indeed a theatre. It is one of the sorrows of my life that I never saw Ellen Terry when she was in full bloom. My only experience of her on the stage was when she played Lady Cicely Waynfleet in Shaw's *Captain Brassbound's Conversion*. Her graciousness led me to suppose that at last Shaw had created for us a woman of nature, breeding and wit. The illusion was momentary; on the whole Stevenson was right when, writing of the few early works of Shaw he had seen, he ejaculated, "My God, what women!"

It is probable that my upbringing in the theatre was bad. I supped full of melodrama. People who can sit silently nowadays through the average film are at a loss to understand why audiences at the old melodramas could watch and listen without ribaldry. We—that is the mass of us—attended pit and gallery much as the groundlings went to *Hamlet*, enjoying the melodrama of it; for we can be sure that the Elizabethan groundlings didn't get as far as the poetry. A drawing in *Punch* of the 'nineties depicted a gallery girl sobbing her heart out while her young man is saying, " 'Ere, Liza, don't tike on so—it isn't reel, reely." And Liza replies, " You leave me alone ; I'm enjoying myself." In the greatest of melodramas, *The Silver King*, which is the compendium of all its kind, summing-up all the unities of melodrama, every convention and device, from a hero guiltless in the end of the murder it seems certain he has committed, to " peculiar whistles " in dark wharves of the Thames —in this masterpiece there was a scene where the heroine is confronted by the landlord, who threatens ejection if she doesn't at once pay up weeks of " back rent." Wilfred Denver, to escape the hangman, has gone to Nevada ; the heroine is left behind in a cottage supposedly impoverished ; but it always had a comfortable southerly aspect with roses in the garden. Well, the landlord arrives in a dreadful rage and bangs the table. Unless the arrears are immediately settled out she must go, child and all. And at the crucial moment Jaikes comes forward, butler at the Old Manor Hall who has known Master Wilfred since he was " so 'igh." He comes forward, bent and frail, holding a bag which he shakes to let us hear the golden coins jangling inside. He hands it to our heroine and says, " Miss, if I may make so bold, a lifetime's savings are at your disposal." She seizes the bag, thrusts it in front of the landlord on the table, then pointing to the door and drawing herself up proud but stern, she declaims, " There, you dastardly man—there's your money—*take it and go* ! " And the audience roared out its approbation—a good number in it no doubt quickly seeing the point, themselves being considerably behind with the rent. The landlord, who after all had merely been seeking his due rather belatedly, shared the evening's hisses from pit and gallery, hisses usually reserved for the accredited villain; and a superb villain he was in *The Silver King*, called "The Spider," played with genius by E. S. Willard. Yes, the melodramas of old were acted by great players, Burbages of a later day. It may be, then, because I was not weaned from melodrama until the advanced age of eighteen or so, that to-day I prefer *Macbeth* to *Back to Methuselah*, and yesteryear was in a minority amongst mature playgoers in regarding *The Second Mrs. Tanqueray* as a better play than, say, *The Voysey Inheritance*.

I am not here arguing that all the arts of the theatre should aspire to the condition of melodrama. Comedy must emerge from another source altogether. But great tragic acting should begin from a recollection in tranquillity of traditional types going as far back as Punch and Jack Ketch. Comedy in our old melodramas was introduced only as relief from severe emotional tension. Wilfred Denver, horrified to find himself submerged in circumstantial evidence of murder, goes down on his knees and, addressing Providence as well as the vast circumference of the theatre, cries out, "O God, put back Thy Universe and give me yesterday!"—after which the scene changes at once to the cook's kitchen where the policeman flirts with her; or the necessary catharsis was performed by a comic drunk trying to buy a ticket at a railway station.

The cinema has taken the place of the old melodrama and farce as the day's normal diet of theatre for the millions. I will make no comment on this change and substitution; I never go to the films except to see the greatest of all comic actors, now or ever, Charlie Chaplin. I have remembered for a while the pleasures of going to melodrama first to amuse myself, then to point a moral; nearly all the great actors I have seen in England have directly or indirectly had training or acquaintance, in some shape, with melodrama, Henry Arthur Jones, Melville—or Shakespeare.

The first concern of any creative artist should be to suit his conceptions to his medium, to expand and glorify and give the medium every possible chance. A play must be of the theatre, not only revelling in the theatre's atmosphere, but taking breath and being from it; and it must, as Mr. Crummles pointed out, bring out the full strength of the company. It must lend scope for histrionics.

The irony of the English stage in our time is that it is Shaw, not Barrie, who can be called " The Playwright that wouldn't grow up." For all Barrie's dreadful mawkishness and his mother-complexes and what-not, life lined his art, so that through the recurrent sentimental puerilities comes the hint of tragic experience. There is at least no briskness in Barrie. He was fortunate to be a *genius* of the theatre and so could wink at the requirements of sophistry of intellectual necessity. I once stayed in his flat near the Adelphi Terrace and he showed me his books, and when he waved his hand to a section of the Scottish Metaphysicians, studied earnestly in his youth, he suddenly broke into a convulsion of mirth that shook his great head and his diminutive body through and through. He told me that for weeks he had worried his brain to make Mary Rose vanish plausibly, in the island scene. He thought of gauze curtains lowered from the " flies " ; he even thought of trap-doors. Then he decided just to let her walk off the stage in full view of the audience—but while Simon is absorbed in putting out the fire and the ghilly is attending to the boat. I do not think I could sit again through *Mary Rose* without some shudderings ; but I am certain I couldn't see the curtain rise on the empty house of the first scene of Act I without a creeping of the spine. Simple genius, to evoke the air and odour of bodeful inexplicable doings, at the same time evoke that pervading pathos which is all the spectral memories flitting about an old house, now vacant, with a dead past, once the place of light and life and happiness and sorrow. Without a word Barrie conjures his dramatic setting, his own unities, in an incomprehensible thaumaturgy of the stage. Our intellect may do its worst in sardonic or outraged protest against Barrie's many disgusting wallowings in sensibility—(it is a common error to suppose that Barrie was prone to sentimentality as it is commonly known. It was a mawkishness of fancy, a prettifying of sympathetic imagination)—as when, for example, Mary Rose talks to the rowan tree on the island after she returns to it ; or when—ugh !—Barrie counters Peter Pan's move to keep the children—Peter flies before them to the house of the Darlings ; he closes the window, then Barrie makes Mrs. Darling in another room play " Home Sweet Home " on the piano, and exhibits to Peter, watching through the door, the tears falling down the mother's cheeks while she cries out "Wendy! Wendy!" It is unfair to Peter, and unspeakably cheap; yet somehow it is not vulgar, only an underhand attack on our superior and grown susceptibilities. And the man who could perpetrate such stuff could enrich us with Hook and Smee, the best parts of *The Admirable Crichton*, and *The Twelve-Pound Look*. The first act of *What Every Woman Knows* is the most brilliant since Sheridan; and even *Dear Brutus* is compact of the stuff which talent dare not handle for a moment.

The course of talent is predictable; and we can by analysis find out whence it has come, and how it has been developed. Genius is unique and not always rational, and is indifferent to contemporary taste and liable to take our breath away and make nonsense of our theories about its next move. Barrie was a "sport," an *isolated* visitation for a given time; none the less he belonged to the theatre and enlarged its scope for magical illusion and for the embodying, through the agency of the old stock-in-trade of stage properties and effects, strange and fascinating shapes and places and people.

It is possible that by some miscalculation of emphasis I have given in this chapter a wrong impression of my appreciation of Shaw in the theatre. I have enjoyed him there with a champagne feeling in my laughter; Shaw is enjoyable anywhere up to a point. But on the stage I wish to enjoy actors as much as I enjoy Shaw; I can after all enjoy actors when I see and hear Shakespeare, Molière, Ibsen, O'Neill, Barrie, and O'Casey. Opportunity for great acting occurs in *Saint Joan* because, as I say, behind Shaw there is a legendary figure to be seized on by the imagination even before Shaw begins. There will always be room for the play of satire and exposure; but it will not endure over a stretch of time unless the characters in it live in their own rights by a volition that leaves the satire far behind. Tartuffe is nowadays interesting for the nature that is in the man, and for the fact that a great actor is needed to unfold Tartuffe; he is not just an indictment of hypocrisy, any more than Mr. Squeers, who had one eye only, though the general prejudice is in favour of two, is primarily an exposure of the brutal schoolmasters of the period.

Round about 1919 I helped with the dramatic criticism on the *Manchester Guardian*, and I quickly realised that the dramatic critic's life is boring compared with that of the music critic. Admitted that the music critic is expected to listen once a month to the fifth symphony of Beethoven and the "Pathétique" of Tchaikovsky and the third Brandenburg Concerto of Bach; still these works are at any rate the products of genius. The average "new" play is not even talented or adult. The music critic is kept in touch with large and creative minds; the dramatic critic may well yawn through twenty successive nights of banal thought and emotion. When we come to think of it, there are few masterpieces of the theatre that will bear perpetual acquaintance, measured with the masterpieces of music, painting and literature. I could easily compile a list of a hundred large-scale compositions with which we are able to live delightedly for a lifetime. How many plays could likewise be chosen?—excepting poetic drama (that is, all drama which aspires to the condition of music and deals first with the emotions in terms of character and only second with a didactic criticism of manners or society). I question whether, beginning from Ibsen, a dozen such masterpieces have been written. *Uncle Vanya*, *The Cherry Orchard*, *The Seagull* are not plays of argument and idea; the stuff of them is poetry, always reaching towards music and sentiment (remember the cadence of "autumn roses, lovely mournful roses"). The old melodramas had the root of the matter in them when at times the action called for "incidental" music.

There is certainly room for all sorts; I would not go as far as Arthur Symons, who maintained "Nothing but beauty should exist on the stage," and that "visible beauty comes with the ballet, an abstract thing; gesture adds pantomime, with which drama begins; and then words bring in speech by which life tries to tell its secret. Because poetry, speaking its natural language of verse, can let out more of that secret than prose, the great drama of the past has been mainly drama in verse."

A rigid application of this theory of the stage would deprive us of many—though maybe not very many—felicities of comedy and wit. But until the theatre is again as dependent on as large a range of great virtuoso acting as the masterpieces of Bach, Mozart, Beethoven, Berlioz and Wagner are dependent on a large range of great and virtuoso instrumentation, I shall for the most part prefer to cherish my memories of those raptures (immature and pagan, I regret to say) provoked in my breast when after we had waited in the queue for the shilling pit for hours, there began the slow progress in file to the penal-looking ticket-office, in front of which some fool would be sure to fumble with his money or want small change and hold us all up exasperatingly, till at last the sudden looming before us of the theatre's interior, the fireproof curtain not raised yet and covered with coloured advertisements in squares, and behind it a world waiting larger than lifesize, presided over by the true and only spirits of the stage—suspense, expectation, and what's to come next!

* VIII *

I HAVE never been ambitious. I have found enjoyment step by step on the roadway of my life and have had no time to think of any sort of goal. But after I had reached the late twenties, as soon as I could open a bank account, I was visited by a wish to go to Savile Row and buy a suit there. I needed to wait, of course, until I could own a cheque-book, because if you pay them in cash in Savile Row they are likely to feel hurt.

So when the time came I went one morning to Savile Row. The first tailor's establishment I came to displayed a crest of the Royal Family "by appointment." I saw just beyond the open and yet exclusive portal a man in striped trousers and a morning-coat; he gave me one glance and that was quite enough. I passed on, pretending I hadn't been looking. The next establishment was as forbidding; the King of Spain bought his clothes there. And so on; the street was like the Almanach de Gotha in procession. I was discouraged until right at the end of the street I came upon a mere shop. It could announce nothing better than the patronage of a Prince of Monaco or some such. So I entered bold as Manchester brass.

A man approached me; he, too, wore the garments and air of an important personage in the Foreign Office and for a while I lost nerve and felt I had been decoyed. I asked him to let me see "something," and he beckoned a hireling who produced a roll of "material," wound round a length of wood. The man from the Foreign Office seized it and hurled a wave of blue serge over the counter and began pulling and snapping at it, making bad-tempered noises, as though he didn't think much of it. It seemed good stuff to me but I didn't want to embarrass him so I asked for another pattern. And the counter was then swamped by a whole Atlantic Ocean of sumptuous cloths, and he tore at all of them, but in vain. At last I made a choice; he obviously didn't approve but I was obstinate. He made another sign of command, this time into the darkest interior, and another hireling appeared, carrying a tape measure. He attacked me with the tape measure and the other hireling got a pencil and a notebook. The tape measure moved and flashed about me so quickly that the man might easily have been tying me into a bundle. I was nervous when his top hand went near the tenderest part of my body but he was gentle as a lamb. When they had finished with me I was asked my address, and I gave the name of my Club, not without a triumphant inflection.

In a fortnight I went for my first "trying-on." The Foreign Office recognised me at once and a command was telephoned upstairs, and after a reasonable interval another hireling, this time his mouth full of pins—and they were also sticking out all over him—appeared before me carrying the vestiges of creation. They seemed to me fairly well advanced, not entirely organic or homogeneous but approximating to the design envisaged. It was suggestive of the sort of blue-print Almighty God might have worked from at his first efforts towards the shape of a human. I was taken into a private cell, and the jacket was put on me, held together it seemed by brown paper and long, loose, badly-sewn cotton. But it fitted, with one or two impatiently jerked adjustments by the Foreign Office, who now began to assert himself and brought out from his pocket a square thin piece of chalk and began sadistically to slice my body with it, sometimes going over the same line twice. Then he abruptly and without warning tore the jacket to ribbons, ripping right and left without mercy. In a moment the thing was in shreds and ribbons, which he handed over to the hireling with the pins in his mouth. " Call in again," he remarked, " next week, say Thursday afternoon at three."

Next week, punctually, I was in Savile Row once more. I was led to the private cell, and after a pause the finished article, as I imagined, was presented to me to get into ; the Foreign Office and assistants retired outside while I dressed in front of a mirror. At a given signal from me, they entered to survey their handiwork. It was too beautiful really, I thought ; I couldn't possibly wear it amongst my friends without fair notice ; I would have to break it gently to them by, say, appearing first of all only in the trousers, then working up to the polished ensemble. I confess I felt vain and self-conscious as the F.O. and his assistant inspected me, walking round me, and giving me prods and pulls behind the back, and fetching me up straight by a tug of the collar.

But the Foreign Office was still bad tempered. As though a rush of blood had come to his head, he yet again fell upon me and with one reckless tug he pulled my arm off, or really it was the arm of the jacket. Then he amputated the other, tearing savagely. And after that he laid his two hands on the lapels on the breast and split them asunder. Before I could utter a word of remonstrance or horror the jacket was a ruin. Nobody seemed able to make a move to stop him. He gave the remnants to the man with the pins and said to me, " Will next Wednesday morning at eleven be convenient for you ? "

Wednesday arrived, as usual. When I went into the cubicle, only the Foreign Office accompanied me, and now he carried almost with some interest the consummated suit. After I had dressed he came to view it. He walked this side and that and swung me round and round. He retired a pace, moved forward and patted my left shoulder. He retired again and looked hard at me. I thought he was about to fling himself at me again and I prepared to defend myself. But no, he even smiled and approved. Nothing was mentioned of price or payment. I instinctively knew that it would be bad taste to bring the matter up. The suit duly appeared at my home. My wife adored it. " Just shows you," she said, " there's something, after all, in going to Savile Row." I went out in it after dark, to begin with. I grew bolder and next day ventured into broad daylight. Nobody said anything at all, until one morning, the third time that I manifested myself in a bloom and glory of brown, my wife, while sitting at lunch with me, asked, " Is that your new suit or the old one ? "

There was a time in this land when only the aristocracy could choose and afford to dress shabbily, on Sundays at any rate. Even the town mechanic or the country labourer was expected, sooner or later in the afternoon, to put on his " Sunday best," which meant a stiff collar if he wished to go out into the world where he was known, and was not content to lie prone from morning till night on the sofa reading the *News of the World* in his shirt and braces. I once lay recumbent myself through a whole Sunday until dark because my trousers, my only trousers, needed some far-reaching repairs. I didn't read the *News of the World* but Robert Louis Stevenson's *Treasure Island*. My age at the time was eighteen, and I haven't picked up *Treasure Island* since, though I went through it at a sitting, or a lying-in; to-day I remember nothing of the story except the " men on a dead man's chest " and the tap-tap of Pew's walking-stick.

Rations temporarily saved us from the martyrdom to the shabby-genteel. There is no call now for paper collars. I wore one of these makeshifts or imitations—an india-rubber collar which would wash every evening, but never was it quite white in the end, or in the beginning. As I was only an office boy, my collar was of the kind called " Eton," very broad and towering to a pyramid. I used to put my trousers under the bed mattress and obtained a different crease every morning. Also I made use of Blakey's Protectors, a metallic device shaped like the half-moon, which was nailed into the soles and heels of one's boots, at points and places where great strain needed to be borne.

I bought my first suit by "easy payments" from what was known as "a Scotchman," meaning somebody named Abrahams or Rosenheim, who called every week at one's home or lodgings to collect the shilling. He took me one Sabbath morning into the ghetto of Cheetham Hill in Manchester, where he had arranged to let me see some patterns and meet the tailor himself. I had never before been to Cheetham Hill on a Sunday and I was fascinated by the sudden transition from Manchester's main vistas of vacancy and respectable inanimation to a week-day activity and trafficking; shops open and very old men in tall hats and long patriarchal beards, walking with their hands clasped behind them, and children playing openly in the streets. My Scotchman took me into a back alley, up a flight or two of stairs, into a long workroom where Jews of all ages sat on the floor, legs astraddle, sewing and cutting. The master tailor approached us and greeted my Scotchman affably and received me with effusion. He showed me a cloth; it was a check as spacious and resonant as any I had ever seen; but I dared not say so, though I was bold enough to insist that I didn't quite like it. The master tailor, named Guggenheimer, was stung to the quick. He fondled the cloth. "But id is be-yootiful," he blubbered, "id is a shame—Oi! Oi!—for dirdy-five shiddings, and 'e says he doessed like id!" Tears came into his eyes, and I hadn't the heart to hold out. The checks were duly made to resemble a suit—an ideal suit for one of the music-hall comedians of the period, one of the red-nosed succession like Harry Champion, who sang songs beginning " O me mother-in-law's come to stay the week." The first time I wore this suit, under cover of a Manchester fog, I ripped the back of the coat on a nail on the back of a chair. On the whole I was relieved, though it was all very tragic for me ; Abrahams had to be paid his weekly instalment just the same. But I remember the experience with pleasure. " Oi ! Oi ! —for dirdy-five shiddigs ad 'e say 'e doessed like id. Oi ! Oi ! " It sounded almost like the lamentations of a cantor in a neighbouring synagogue.

The Sabbath of my boyhood remained a terror to the young in Christian English homes. Small boys, even in the working classes, as I have said, were put into strange and restrictive garb. I remember a black velvet sailor suit, a lanyard, short white socks that wouldn't stay up, and a sailor hat labelled " H.M.S. Benbow." I would not go out in it unless dragged by force, both feet to the ground, like a reluctant puppy. I was afraid of derision from other boys until I saw 'Arry Wilkinson, next door but one, and son of a foreman bricklayer, arrayed in a Scotch kilt. All Sunday we were suppressed, and sent to Sunday school in the afternoon, from which we were expected to bring home texts from the Scriptures printed on small illuminated cards. On the walls of the class-room hung pictures of Cain and Abel, red blood and sand, or of mules carrying bundles tied with rope, or of smoke rising to the sky and white-haired and bearded old men, very vermilion in the face, stretching up their arms ; Moses and rods and more smoke and desert and rock. On Sunday evening English families of the lower orders opened and entered the front room, the parlour, where there was a fireplace brazen with fire-irons, brass tongs and shovel, never used. On the mantelpiece of my home was a photograph of my grandfather, framed in corks, depicting him holding a manuscript clenched in his left hand, apparently about to make a public statement. Also there was a set of lustres and a ship made of glass, enclosed in a globe, frail, lovely and frozen as though lost in an Arctic sea. An evergreen plant stood in the window in a gaudy pot, both received as barter for rags, bones, or some garment discarded at the last.

The rag-and-bone man came round every week, with a donkey drawing his cart, which sometimes was aerial with coloured balloons. They have all passed away; the back-street vendors and itinerants; the knife-grinder, so thrilling to watch as he struck sparks from his swiftly-revolving round stone, worked by his right foot with a treadle; the Italian organ-grinder, bowing himself in two when a penny was thrown out of an upper window, glossy hair and moustaches, swarthy as a gipsy, velvet coat, a picture of the Italian lakes on the front of his instrument, which he played with a handle; and he could change from a left to right grip without spoiling the rhythm or the arpeggio of octaves. And on top of the organ was a monkey, pathetically waiting, looking for something, and, not finding it, scratching himself. As twilight came the lamplighter with his two long poles, one to open the glass door, the other to invoke a glow which in a November fog was yellow and ghostly, and, to my myopic unspectacled eyes, like a great luminous jellyfish, with a black spot in the middle.

All, or nearly all, these workers and mendicants wore clothes telling of their office or function : navvies with string tied towards the bottom of their trousers ; dustmen in corduroy—they could strike matches on their backsides ; butchers in blue aprons ; coachmen in tall hats, with a cockade ; the Jew "mender of windows," sometimes wearing two or three bowler hats, one on top of the other, rather green, and he carried a frame of glass on his back and smelt of putty. And now and again a gipsy knocked at the door to tell the lady's fortune, and she wore large ear-rings and a brilliant scarf round her hair, and she showed white teeth in a smile of irresistible confidence and good will. Soldiers of the period were vivid in shortened coats. There was romance in our back alleys and streets, coats of many colours.

IX

WHEN, in September, 1939, we were all blown about the world like particles in an explosion, I landed first bounce in Australia. The trifler who made his livelihood out of music found himself unemployed; concerts came to an end at the beginning of that first winter of tension and black nights. Cricket, of course, would need no historian for years to come. I was imprisoned in Manchester, useless to anybody. Out of the void came a cable from Sir Keith Murdoch, inviting me to join the staff of the *Melbourne Herald*—no, not as a writer on sport in a land of born players of games, but as music critic.

My home, eventually in Sydney, was a "third floor front" of a block of flats called "West End." It looked upon bricks and mortar, except that a narrow side window allowed a suggestion of Rushcutter's Bay to come shining through the afternoon's fall. On the whole the place was untouched by sun and had the coolness of a cellar in the hot seasons. The main room contained nothing but a bed divan, a table, two or three chairs, a writing-desk, a radio-gramophone and a bookshelf. The colour was brown. Also there were a small kitchen and a very attractive bathroom, black and white. This flat became my ivory tower; only the privileged few entered. Not even my wife dreamed of invasion without giving decent warning. For six years I seldom went out of this hermitage until twilight. Australian summers blazed away; winters set in with August's chill wind and rain. A world war raged, and the destinies of nations went awry. In my solitude I got down each morning to my desk, after preparing my own breakfast of tea, cereals, milk and toast, and after making my own bed, washing-up, and dusting each room; for I would tolerate no invading cleaner for a long time. I found an ironing-board and an electric iron, and because of a stupid strike in Sydney amongst laundry-men I determined to attend to my own linen and suit-pressing. This recreation enabled me to think out ideas, and only once did my technique, which soon operated automatically, go wrong, leaving on one of my shirts the imprint of a brown and passionate heart.

One day I remained at my desk from ten until five, interrupted by ten minutes or so at noon for a drink and a sandwich. I produced four or five thousand words of my *Autobiography* in this time; and my Aunt Beatrice walked into the book and threatened to play everybody else, myself first of all, off the stage. I had to "kill" her, which I did sadly enough, saying to her, "But, my dear, it's my autobiography I'm writing, not your biography." "Change it to a novel," she implored, "and let me be the heroine." I was adamant, perhaps mistakenly so. This was a day of ecstasy for me such as I had never before experienced. That evening, when I went out into the streets and saw the world and all its busyness again, and when I read something momentous about one Mussolini, I could almost feel my eyes and my mind blinking as my consciousness made a difficult adaptation. I was, they will say, an escapist. On the contrary, I was being impelled for the first time in my life into reality as an artist; that is, I was impelled neck-high into work which imperatively demanded devotion to the muse and forgetfulness of self. For a period I hated this discipline of daily devotion. I had so far been a journalist, a music critic, drawing my honey from flowers to be found everywhere; in other words, a job of work had to be done needing only the necessary tricks of the trade. I had written no books, as books; my publications so far were collected articles from the *Manchester Guardian*. It was a different matter, then, to sit down before blank paper, pads of it, with—so to say—nowhere, or worse still, *everywhere*, to go. There was almost a lifetime's habit to break as a preliminary, and I needed to free myself from the tyranny of the newspaper column. I had been trained for the "distance" of twelve hundred words; my conceptions naturally shaped themselves to the printed column's scope. When I began my *Ten Composers* I was dismayed that I could not at first stay a longer course than a thousand or so words; I had to put myself through an entirely new training.

I suffered much. I have walked round that room in "West End" in circles of aching despair. I have sat at the desk hours and not put a word on to paper. One day revelation was vouchsafed me. The great thing, I discovered, was the devotion, the wooing of the muse.

No matter how barren the morning of words written, I was enabled to rise from my seat and rest cramped fingers and put down my pen with a feeling of rare inward peace. I realised that the muse will not respond if you court her only in her bountiful hours. She has her pride. She wants the sign of faith; she wants to be taken for better or worse. She will give much in return for a love of her that is for her own sake, in pregnancy and even when the "curse" is on her.

I came to a dead end in the essay on Elgar in my *Ten Composers*—Elgar of all men; I had imagined he would "write himself." But no; for a month I was stuck. By chance—or *do* these illuminations come by hazard?—I turned to the passage in the *Conversations with Goethe*, where Goethe warns writers against impatience. "We must be right by nature so that good thoughts may come before us like free children of God, and cry 'Here we are!'" The impediment in my Elgar essay was presently removed.

As I say, my problem was to develop staying-power over a distance longer than the newspaper column. I believe in the relation of function to structure. In all the arts the idea itself, the thing seeking expression, can easily change according to the urgencies or requirements of form. As David Balfour said to himself, when he heard Alan Breck singing the song of his own composition which praised the victory over the enemy in the siege of the Round House and did not award David a place in the pæan, "but poets (as a very wise man once told me) have to think upon their rhymes." The solemnity of thought of a Beethoven adagio was probably not infrequently a consequence of the effect of form upon a mind not necessarily solemn at the moment, or at the outset of the execution of a job to be done.

In other words, I was compelled to learn a new medium, or, rather, how to modulate as well as sustain. At the age of fifty, after nearly a quarter of a century's experience on a paper of the literary standards of the *Manchester Guardian*, I had to practise writing—practise it exactly as a pianist practises on his instrument. I would give an hour to exercises, to the filling of pages, not to " say " anything, and knowing well that I would scrap the lot. The object was to acquire a fresh rhythm and, as musicians would say, to acquaint myself with subtler tonalities, more evocative contrasts, and changes of key.

In the end the writer must use his palette of language instinctively. Samuel Butler maintained that no writer ever wrote well who thought much about " style." I would argue that nobody has written to his own or anybody else's satisfaction without deliberately practising a style intuitively selected, and mastering it until it will work by itself, and become subdued to what it works in.

With none but a journalist's practice, a writer is no more likely to produce a shapely book than a jockey skilled in flat-racing is likely to prosper at a steeplechase. And in the long run what counts most of all is subconscious memory, reflected experience. My first experiment in my ivory tower was *Ten Composers*, which obsessed me for three years. But though while at work on it, frequently held up and always under the delusion that ideas and sentences were coming to me as children fresh from God, I realised when I read it after I had finished, that it contained scarcely anything that I had not written in Hallé concert notices for the *Manchester Guardian* years earlier. Frequently, in fact, I repeated word for word an impression received " on the night ; " yet I had " hammered it out " page by page as though for the first time in the throes of delighted and surprising and arduous creative activity. A curiosity for the psychologist is that in the Elgar essay I repeated a paragraph from Samuel Langford almost without the alteration of a comma ; but as I wrote down the words they were my own, a blessed visitation. The passages are as follows :

From Langford's *Musical Criticisms :*

" Here, in these works " [Elgar's at a Three Choirs Festival], " we have known music, as music everywhere ought to be—an art indigenous, creative, serious, free and life-quickening. . . . The consciousness that an art has grown up to maturity, from the very ground you are treading, and is bearing its blossom and its fruit all around you, is something different from the feeling that it has been brought to you from a very long way. . . ."

From *Ten Composers* :

" Here, at the harvest of the year in country washed by the rivers of the West, we have known music as music everywhere should be ; part of the soil, creative, free, serious, life-giving. The thought that an art has grown up from the very ground you are treading and is bearing its fruit all around you is something different from the feeling that it has been brought to you from a long way. . . ."

Here is an example of the workings of unconscious plagiarism that is an eloquent tribute to Langford's influence on me, a proof of how deep into my heart and mind went the roots of his conversations with me. Two or three years passed by after the publication of *Ten Composers* before I noticed the resemblance, or let us call it, the reincarnation.

It is wise for writers on completing a manuscript to put it away in a drawer for six months at least; when they look at it again they can, or should be able to, see it objectively, as though the work of somebody else. I subjected *Ten Composers* to this test of probation, and to my astonishment I felt a change of tempo and choice and colour of words in each chapter as another theme or composer was treated. The essays on Strauss and Wagner are at times reckless and purpled; Schubert is discussed youthfully and yet not, I think, callowly. Sibelius thins out my prose to (for me) a quite rationed austerity. I wrote the César Franck fantasy like a man who willingly surrenders reason and the logic of the head to the impulses of the heart and the authority of visions. The comparisons with the poetry of Herbert, and also the metaphor describing Franck's harmonic and cyclic method: "His art is a perpetual transubstantiation of music. Out of three chromatic notes he frames not a fourth sound, but a star. Prelude Aria and Finale. Prelude Chorale and Fugue . . . God is One and God is Three. . . ."—I cannot give to-day to such writing the support of the rational intellect. I would not have risked this way the immolation of my critical and mundane self had I been writing in London, where the pressure of a sophisticated environment discourages flights into the beatific, the uncharted and possibly inane imaginative territory. But the Franck essay was not deliberately written, not the consequence of virtuosity and consciously sought allusions. It "wrote itself," and I shall not forget the happiness that possessed me from outside of me, as I sat in the third floor front on a morning of Easter, with the Australian sun flaming through my window, and all Sydney out of town, the streets more or less silent and empty.

The risks to be taken with writing of this sort are terrible. But I cannot think that any writer will profit by timidity and inhibitions if he feels grace is descending on him. I assume, of course, that he is anchored to earth by some knowledge, sense of humour and proportion. It is simply that he is bound to accept the cornucopia of the muse full to the brim; he will be a fool to pick and choose, and may also end in foolishness if he humbly, gratefully, and with some embarrassment, accepts the lot. He must take the chance—take it or leave it. He will miss much of joy by caution and, no doubt, will continue to appeal to common sense.

To write about César Franck at all in a Sydney flat was for me an "experience"; to hear from the gramophone the aspiring phrases of the beginning of the piano quintet, in a land still too sane, too clear-cut of outline and too oblivious of inner dissonances of spirit! The room at 35 West End is to-day surely full of sweet sounds when it is empty; and at least one ghost will be seen or heard in it some night. I wonder if the carpet has been changed where, under my desk I would put my feet, so that in six years I wore it threadbare. . . .

I have had my annunciatory moments in No. 35. One summer afternoon towards evening I played records of the Requiem of Fauré; and after the music came to a close the place was quieter than ever. The tall and gracious gladioli pointed upwards like candles; the afterglow of the sun stained the brickwork of the houses outside to a texture suggesting peach-bloom; from the window the spire of the church near Rushcutter's Bay seemed more than still; it was as though arrested and isolated from time and space. On my writing-desk my white cat shaped out of porcelain stared with eyeless sight into a void. I came now as near as ever in my life to the peace that passeth all understanding. I nearly saw God, but not quite. It is as well that He shows us no more than His hinder parts; for if ever He were to reveal to us His full countenance there would be an end to faith and the meaning and the inspiration of faith. We mustn't be hot for certainties in this our life.

The remarkable gifts of Australia for music have been quickened by the Jews that came from Europe to escape or avoid Hitler. Even as Manchester received the foundations of its music from German Jews in the 'sixties, 'seventies, and 'eighties, so, it may well occur, will Australia enjoy a like cultural transfusion. Amongst these exiled Europeans was Ignaz Friedman, nearly the last Grand Seigneur of the piano (never famous in

England, where some domesticity at the instrument is considered reassuring on the whole), but honoured throughout the Continent as man and artist. For six years he was a joy of my life in Sydney ; witty, a man of the world, yet a thinker, genial but ironic, philosophical in conversation but often afflicted by simple, lovable vanities in the everyday traffic of life. Nobody has played the smaller pieces of Chopin with quite Friedman's touch and absorption. His interpretation of the Mazurkas were legend and history rendered into tone. He would play the postlude to a mazurka as though reluctant to take leave of the music ; his fingers seemed to contain throbs of fancy, love and relish, straight from his mind. He could convince me for a while of the greatness of the B minor sonata of Liszt. It was in his hands grand in rhetoric ; also it was of the right faded sentiment ; the aroma and flavour of the burnt cigar, of astrakhan and dandruff, and thick curtains still not drawn next morning. He was the best I have known at telling a story. His face became histrionic, with a Grimaldi droop of the mouth. His masterpiece was his account of his appearance at a Sydney police station when it was necessary for him to register, in war-time, as an alien. He appeared before a policeman who sat at a small table upon which his helmet reposed ; for the morning was hot.

"Name ?"

"Friedman."

"Howjer spell it ?"

Friedman asked for a pencil. "I will write it down for you."

The constable inspected the signature.

"Fried—man? Huh. And what's your first, your Christian name?"

"Ignaz—also I spell it for you—so."

The constable again pored over the signature, then spoke again.

"What are yer?"

Friedman was here naturally a little at a loss.

"What am I?—pleas' explain."

"I mean what *are* yer, whadjer do for a livin'."

"Oh," collaborated Friedman, "I am a pianist."

"Pianist?"

"Yes."

"Yer meanter say yer play the pianner?"

Friedman murmured a modest affirmative. The constable pondered again, then said:

"And where jer play?"

Friedman didn't wish to bring in the suspect names of Berlin, Vienna and Rome at such a moment, so he replied:

"Brisbane, Sydney——"

"What? You've played in public in Sydney and Brisbane?"

"Yes."

"Anywhere else?"

"Yes, Melbourne, Adela-ide" (pronounced as the Germans pronounce the name of Beethoven's song), "Tasmania——"

"So you plyed the pianner in all these plices?"

He went into a deeper than ever session of silent thought, before abruptly and rather officiously asking:

" Who's yer boss ? "

Friedman lived in a house high up at Vaucluse on the edge of the sea. Every Tuesday evening I would visit him, and he greeted me with sherry, until by doctor's commands he was forced into total abstinence at last. Neuritis made the fingers of the left hand helpless. Once I asked him if there were signs of improvement.

" No. It is six months since I have played. If I put a threepenny piece into my palm I do not know, if I do not look, that it isn't two shillings, which would not be good for a Jew. Yes ; six months and I do not play. But you, my dear Cardus—every morning I read in the *Sydney Herald* that you have praised celebrated pianists who also play only with the right hand."

His wife, Mania, a niece of Tolstoy, was as great in her way as Friedman in his ; and it was a divertingly different way. She was devoutly religious ; what is more, of the Orthodox Church. Friedman was an atheist. Mania was anti-Semite in many of her views ; Friedman, a Polish Jew, was a " good European." Mania was loquacious and of immense gusto. Friedman possessed the concentration and precision which comprise three parts of wit. One evening Mania left the dinner-table, where she served gargantuan and luscious dishes of her own cooking, to attend to a call on the telephone. She was absent for three-quarters of an hour. When she returned, Friedman looked at his watch and said, " But, Mania, how *can* you speak on the telephon' for so long ?—three-quarters of an hour ; it is not possible." Mania, haughty as Catharine, put up her snub nose. " I haf my friends ; I can always speak to my friends. . . ."

Soon there was another ring. This time Mania was absent from the table for ten minutes, and Friedman greeted her return triumphantly :

" Ach ; only now ten minutes ; you make an epigram on the telephon', so ? "

Mania one night burst indignantly into the artists' room at a concert in Melbourne during the first interval. " Ignaz," she protested. " You bring me to a barbar' country. For while *you* play Chopin, a man in the audience, next to me, sleeps. God in heaven ! He sleeps while Friedman plays ! "

" Mania," said Friedman, " it is always good to sleep."

In the glow of the room in the house at Vaucluse, with the rain and wind of a winter night so wild that during a lull we could hear the thunder of the sea, Friedman's talk was as good as, if not better than, the red wine ; for though there are excellent burgundies in Australia, they are, like the country itself, rather lacking in vintage. (" Good in its way," as the Scottish merchant said to Professor George Saintsbury when discussing a Richebourg, " but it's a coorse wine ! ") And Mania would ply her needles to the socks, and in the benignity of her big-natured compound of patrician and peasant, cultured woman and hoydenish lover of fun, the evening basked ; the three of us, far away from our homelands, remote at the earth's other end, the old world changing hour by hour. But now I felt none of that irony of passing time I had experienced when sitting with little

Max, in another existence. There were no ghosts here to remind us of the vanishing hours. There are no ghosts in Australia yet. . . . Perhaps one or two will appear before long in the Village Lower Road of Vaucluse: a white-headed young-old man, waving good-bye after midnight to his guest, lighting the descending steps to the garden gate then closing the door, leaving the guest in the darkness to grope his way uphill in the teeth of the gale, to wait for a tram for an hour perhaps, alone in the night, but flushed with good food, drink, and contact with genius, flushed too by the sense of the fact that it was here, alone in the night in Sydney, in wind and rain, that he was waiting.

It wouldn't occur to Friedman to ring up a taxi garage for me. He wasn't mean, far from it; but he never forgot that as a young man he wore away his eyes copying music for a pittance. "Don't waste money," he once warned me. "I will tell you a moral. When I was a leetle boy in Poland, my old mother came to me and said, 'Ignaz, my son'—and she strokes my hair —'Ignaz, listen, my son. Soon I go avay; I am old, and God will take me. Then you vill be alone in the vorlt. So I speak to you now good advice. Listen, Ignaz: Ven anybody vants to give you anything—take, take, take. Votever it is, old pieces of string or tin cans —take, my son, take. But'—and she clasps me to her heart, 'but, Ignaz; if anybody vants to take anything from you—call for the po-lice.'"

He was not happy in Australia and died an exile.

But for my own part I found, I repeat, in my third

floor front in Sydney the solitude that is good for a man in his middle years who has lived (and loved) and needs to "overhaul his catechism." In Australia, I worked not only as a music critic and a broadcaster on music—a weekly Sunday talk of an hour's length, with illustrations. In seven years I also produced four books. As a friend of mine wrote to me from London, "Apparently at last you have found nobody who you can talk to or who will listen to you—so you are talking to yourself." In other words, writing books. In addition, I enjoyed myself in a land where it is as natural for people to be happy and friendly as it is for the sun to shine.

X

AT the end of my seventh year in Sydney I was reminded, in the words of Vanderdecken, that the term was over; "der Frist ist um." I was in need of spiritual replenishment from London; so on a windy morning I flew home from Rose Bay.

I reached Poole on an afternoon of spring. A car drove us to the railway station at Bournemouth, and we went along roads lined with trees in the green bud. A tall elderly man, with eyeglasses attached to his person by a thick ribbon, turned in his walk to call a dog. This was the beginning of my sentimental journey. There was a Pullman car waiting at the station. There were white tablecloths, gleaming cutlery, knives, forks and spoons, which made the old tinkle as the train got into motion. The attendant of the dining-car came forward and asked, "Would you care for an aperitif, sir?" He served a sourish sherry, and afterwards, a dinner which was potential rather than real. But the gesture of it all, the politeness, the simulation of some art and elegance of living, touched me as much as it delighted and amused me. Then, in the twilight of London Town, I drove in a taxi to my club and saw Whitehall, and caught a glimpse of the Thames. As soon as I entered the club and went to the office to report my arrival, Frank himself greeted me. "Good evening, sir," he said, "back again. There's some letters waiting for you." A direct hit from a bomb had destroyed the club's main staircase. Worlds had been thrown into the melting-pot. But there were letters waiting.

I had flown from Italy at the dawning of the same day, bringing with me wine and cigars for James Agate. After I had gone to my room and washed and changed, I telephoned to Agate; but there was no answer to the "buzz-buzz" of my call. I concluded that he was at a theatre. Next morning as I lay in bed with my tea and toast, I read in *The Times* that he was dead, and had given up his restless ghost almost at the moment I was trying to ring to him the evening before.

As I walked the old familiar places in London I was brought many times to the edge of tears in indefinable ways. The sight of young girls emerging from the offices and shops at "rush" hour, each carrying a satchel over the shoulder, hatless and neat and not obviously "glamorous," talking as they walked in twos with that intimacy which is the symbol of girls' freemasonry; and the sight of tired faces of the middle-aged, shabby but respectable in appearance, in buses and tube, concealed behind newspapers—these were manifestations of London and England's persistence through times good and evil. Of not many of these people could it have been said a few years ago that they would be alive the next day. The thought bowled me over, and made me feel I could not be counted one of them. I had missed the initiation.

In St. James's Park, as the sun was setting, the ducks turned upside down in the lake, and a large and rather uncontrolled young Airedale dog leaped aggressively towards a small terrier, but thought better of it when he came within growling distance, and swerved away at a slower pace, as though of his own free will and choice. Lovers sat in the shadows. A policeman walked round a bend in a path at an abrupt angle and saw a youth and girl lost in embrace and surrender. He at once turned on his tracks and disappeared round the same bend. As the glow of the sun faded, and night began to fall, there was the old quacking on the lake, as parent ducks called to young; and here and there, one of these young, almost out of touch with nest and home, would suddenly zigzag across the water at a speed defying human eyesight. There was a multitudinous chattering of birds; "in the osier isle we heard their noise." From the bridge looking towards Whitehall was accumulated nobility of dome and turret vanishing like white ghosts in the sky. The noise of the traffic was now low, and the lights went up along the Mall.

Next day I went to Lord's, where there was no apparent change, except for need of paint. In the Long Room there was silence and polish, as the cricket went an uneventful way, and we looked at it through the pavilion's windows as ever. In the refreshment bar there is a ledge along the wall on which the history of the game is fixed in arrested attitudes by ancient photography. After drink and a sandwich have been obtained you can sit at this ledge and consume them. I took a place next a superbly-preserved member of the

M.C.C.; patrician of nose, and he wore a Winchester tie. He sipped his tea, then drew a small paper bag from his pocket and dropped a lump of sugar into his cup. I couldn't divert my gaze from him in time; he realised he had been seen, and he handed the bag to me, saying, "Would you care for a lump, sir?" At tea, a queue waited to be served in this same bar of the Long Room. I took my stand at the end, and when I had reached second place from the top, the distinguished grey moustached Forsyte in front of me turned and bowed and, motioning me forward, said, "After you, sir." I wondered if I was expected to turn to the man next to me in the queue and say "After *you*, sir"; and if politeness would pass right down to the bottom of the queue with the effect of a row of tin soldiers falling down backwards.

During this sentimental period of the native's return, every incident and scene assumed a new significance; old themes had been orchestrated by history and dire experience. The humour remained incomprehensible to those of other nations. It was at Lord's one Saturday, during the morning of a match between the Army and Navy, a quiet and not densely-populated occasion, that I stood at the bar of the Tavern enjoying a half-pint. I was carrying *The Times Literary Supplement*, folded up, and a man at the counter, in bowler hat and muffler, saw the title. "Excuse me, sir," he said, "but are you interested in literature?" It was a momentous question to cope with, considering the circumstances, so I shrugged my shoulders and murmured something non-committal. But he was not to be put off in this way.

"Tell me," he now asked, "wot d'you think of Milton?" I imagine that an hour of exposition, sociological and metaphysical, would be required to demonstrate to an American in what way the above incident is funny in the slightest.

The old order had not, after all, changed and given place entirely to the new. As the flood gradually subsided, after the deluge, the old social contours and lines of demarcation could be faintly discerned again, through the settling waters. *The Times* remained *The Times*, and the "Proms" the "Proms." Ernest Newman, scholarly and witty as ever, and still throwing new light on Wagner in consequence of the discovery of proof that a letter by him to Liszt was written on the 16th of December, 1864, not the 17th as so far generally but mistakenly thought. Agate, alas, no more! but Desmond MacCarthy and Ivor Brown and Kingsley Martin, and Uncle Tom Cobleigh and all, remained in the saddle. The "new" or contemporary generation of weekly reviewers seemed to me callow, and one or two of their elders seemed bored. War had interrupted a tradition; there was missing a "centre" party between extreme Right and Left Wings. The mandarins, as though to assure us or themselves that they were not things of the past, frisked about with the very latest in verse, prose, atonalism and surrealism, like so many old bucks ogling desperately the contemporary scene. I preferred Newman and Agate, who would never desert their Wagners and Sarahs but remained rooted to the soil that nurtured them. The younger scribes, pale from too much education, applied themselves to music, theatre, films "one down, t'other come on" . . . Furtwängler was severely taken to task; one of the B.B.C.'s gallants pointed out to him that the fifth symphony of Beethoven, at the beginning of the first movement, is marked *allegro con brio*. Sophistication walked the town on stilts. Dr. Leavis related Jane Austen to the novel of "significant shape," praised her for "impersonalising her moral tensions," or some such, incidentally dismissing Thackeray and Meredith as triflers who could bring to their material no illuminating form, ethic or æsthetic. Poor Jane! What embarrassment for her modest shade to find an immortality in the company of George Eliot and Henry James!

It was all as diverting to the returning exile as ever; signs of what the biologists call "sports" in the psychology of a nation not ordained, in the beginning, for conscious culture. The normal everyday way of life in England was, as ever, the main and everlasting and organic stem. The ordinary people, without awareness of their responsibility, shouldered the inherited greatness of England.

Our pleasures need cellarage. The grape is not the wine. I will not in this book bring out a new bottle. Time is the winepress; ripeness is all—which is another way of saying that to grow old wisely and well is to understand the perspective of years. Pleasures fit for savouring at the high noon of a full life are to be felt, almost seen, as vistas receding to the past, like avenues in a city at the end of the day, narrowing in twilight mists. By all means let us attend as long as we draw breath to the vineyard of fresh experience, but the fruits must wait in the bin. The gentle irony of the changing seasons and customs is the true vintner.

And the greatest of mellowers is—irony! Without it we remain green in the remembrance of our pleasures. We might as well run about with the crowd, intent on "having a good time," if now and again we do not feel ourselves drawn aside from the show and traffic of things by that disinterested spectator who is always somewhere in us, if we are grown folk at all, and made to realise that beauty vanishes.

We have all suffered from the man who boasts he is as young as anybody, and as modern. He is ready for the newest tipple; his cellar, so to say, is up to date. The latest vintage. "Can't live in the past," he protests. This fool will get nothing even from next year's harvest, let alone from this year's; there is no granary in his mind.

Most people are touchy on three points. You can accuse them of a lack of moral sense. They will shrug shoulders. "Well . . . who of us is?"—with reference to a casting of the first stone. But if you tell them they have no sense of humour they at once get angry and prove that—they haven't. And few, increasingly few these days, will remain calm if you call them old-fashioned.

I confess that I cannot, and would not, deny the age of everything that is in me. Only the very young should be new-fashioned; they can grow out of it. I want always to feel the smack of the salt of years; every one of us, boys and old men alike, are bound to be boring from time to time. It is as well to avoid rawness during the recurrent tedium of living; the old bore has at least some experience which will "break in."

The test of years is everything. A pleasure of a kind known for first the time only yesterday, a new composition, a new book, a new friend, a new anything, will need to survive iteration. Some people, as I say, do not grow old, cannot grow old—like the violin of Heifetz. I am happier with Kreisler's, even when it is slightly out of tune, when it falters in technique and becomes wrinkled with those lines which dignify an ageing face.

Summer after summer up and down England, with my eyes on green grass for hours and my face receiving the brown of sun and air; autumns and Salzburg or Worcester or Gloucester or Hereford for music. Then winter and the Hallé Concerts and Queen's Hall. Thursday in Manchester, back next day in a first-class restaurant car to St. Pancras, arriving in London just in time for cocktail before dinner. Here and there and everywhere—London and Sydney; and as the important musical and cricket events were arranged to take place much at the same dates each season, I could say, "Why, at this very time last twelve months ago I was in this very same place, and next year I shall be here again."

The years flashed by like a kaleidoscope, with one's experiences exquisitely related, each a separate "shot," so to say, in the continuous film of full imaginative living. But—I am asked this question by nearly everybody who meets me for the first time—cricket and music? "How could you mix them?"—with the implication that cricket is, to echo Smee, a bit of a "come-down" for a musical pirate. It is a silly question. As well might a man be asked how can he mix breathing with walking, or wine with song, or George Meredith with gardening, or mountaineering with Wagner. If we are not clods of earth, or worse still, "experts" and "specialists," we will expand our way of life according to where our antennæ of sensibility lead us. I would be an intellectual snob if I were to maintain that I have not loved days at Lord's as intensely as nights at Covent Garden and in both places found in equal abundance material for my writings and—more important—for my memory's granary of good things fully experienced—rich wine of temperament for the day's diet of sights and sounds. Only an æsthete would pretend that an innings by Woolley could not approach as closely to an expression of personal art, plus skill and character, all presented in a significant scene, as the performance of the next fashionable tenor, or somebody's slick, quick exploitation of technique in a Rachmaninoff concerto.

Whether any happening in art or in life is of consequence depends not on the form in which the happening is presented; it depends on our capacity for *experiencing*, on whether our "receiving sets" are sensitively attuned. The silent room we sit in is full of sounds and sweet airs that will give delight and, possibly, hurt not—if the apparatus is there. But most people's lives are like deaf rooms, silent for want of a responsive "pick-up":

. . . Such harmony is in immortal souls ;
But, whilst this muddy vesture of decay
Doth grossly close it in, we cannot hear it.

Did grace fall the more blissfully upon me when I heard the "Echo" nocturne on a summer night at Salzburg while the candles on the music-stands burned steadily, and the stars above were like the pulsation of the notes of Mozart's music? Or when I watched Spooner rippling the sunlit grass with strokes that were without solidity or earthly momentum, and he leaned gracefully forward and flicked his wrists and the whole of the June day and the setting of sky and white tents and the trees of Canterbury were as though the created element of this lovely player's every motion and breath of being? Or when I walked in daylight to Covent Garden, white tie and tails, for all the workaday world to see, on my way from my club for the beginning of the *Ring* at Covent Garden, a leisurely walk along Henrietta Street and through the market, savouring the hour as the sun cast its evening glow on London? Or when I listened to Friedman, then walked soon after under the starry sky of Vaucluse? Or when I heard Toscanini transform an orchestra into shot silk and gold of tone while conducting "Daphnis et Chloe" of Ravel; or when I heard Seth Lomas conducting at a rehearsal the choir in a Lancashire town where the cobbled streets resound at the crack of dawn from the impact of hurrying clogs? It was Christmas time and they were at a "Messiah" practice, and Seth sounded his tuning-fork and the basses made humming noises like wasps; then Seth spoke and said, "And all you open thi mouths. Foller mi beat. And never mind what tha was listenin' to at t' 'Allé Concert last week. It's me that's conducting thi now—not 'Amilton 'Arty."

Only the material, the rare stuff for imagination's manufacture, is given to us, whether by Bach or by the Matterhorn or by César Franck or by the stillness of snow at Christmas or by Dickens or by Harry Dean or Seth Lomas. We must ourselves fashion it into spirit and sensibility and weave it into the texture of our being. Whether the shape or symbol be sonnet or sunset, curve of fiddle-bow or curve of cricket bat, only with our own vision may we see the light and be free to say,

I was for that time lifted above earth,
And possest joys not promised in my birth.

THE END

INDEX